D0775237

THE AGONY OF FREEDOM

How I lost myself in a cult, rebuilt my life, and faced my death with peace

ELIANA BERLFEIN

WITH STACEY STERN

POLKA DOT PRESS   BOULDER | COLORADO

Polka Dot Press
Boulder, CO

Copyright © 2020 Polka Dot Press

All rights reserved. No part of this book may be used in any manner
whatsoever without the written permission of the publisher, except for
brief quotations included in book reviews.

First print edition published in 2020
Printed in the United States of America

Book cover designer: Linda Parks https://parksgroupboulder.com/
Interior designer: Hynek Palatin
Coauthor and editor: Stacey Stern https://staceystern.com/
Proofreaders: Rivvy Neshama and John Wilcockson
https://rivvyneshama.com/editing
https://www.linkedin.com/in/john-wilcockson-5046b912/
Back cover photo of Eliana Berlfein by Nancy November Sloane

Publisher's Cataloging-in-Publication Data
Names: Berlfein, Eliana, 1954-2019, author. | Stern, Stacey, 1966-, coauthor.
Title: The Agony of Freedom: How I lost myself in a cult, rebuilt my life,
    and faced my death with peace / Eliana Berlfein with Stacey Stern.
Description: First print edition. | Boulder, CO: Polka Dot Press, 2020. |
    Summary: *The Agony of Freedom* reveals how Eliana Berlfein
    dropped out of college to spend much of her twenties in Reverend
    Moon's cult, was kidnapped and deprogrammed, battled depression,
    built a new life, learned to love herself, and approached her death
    with peace.
Identifiers: LCCN 2020900816 | ISBN 978-1-7343414-0-9
Subjects: BISAC: BIOGRAPHY & AUTOBIOGRAPHY / Personal
    Memoirs | RELIGION / Cults | PSYCHOLOGY / Psychopathology
    / Depression | BODY, MIND, & SPIRIT / Inspiration & Personal
    Growth | FAMILY & RELATIONSHIPS / General.

For my sisters

Contents

Act Three
The Rest of My Life (1981–2019)

Los Angeles (1981–1985)

Boulder (1985–1988)

San Diego (1988–1996)

Contents

Facing Death (October 29, 2018–January 31, 2019)

Note from the Author

I wrote the first draft of this book in 2002. At the time I simply wanted to tell about my experience of spending six years in a cult followed by the trauma of getting kidnapped out of the Moonies and deprogrammed. After I finished the initial draft, I knew I had to put it aside for a while because I didn't have enough clarity about my life to write the ending.

In 2017 I returned to the original manuscript with two goals in mind. The first was to complete the book for my own personal transformation. Although my time in the Moonies profoundly affected the rest of my life, I felt like I had tucked that period into its own little box, and I wanted to integrate it into the rest of my life. I hoped the process of writing would help me do that.

The second goal was to offer my story as a way to help other people heal from their own troubles. I have dealt with depression throughout my life, and I wanted my struggles to be of value to others. For my book to accomplish that, I knew it must show my own evolution. It had to have three acts— before the cult, during the cult, and, most importantly, my process of healing after the cult. I had a rough draft of acts one and two, but because writing the third act would require a lot of self-reflection, which felt overwhelming, I procrastinated.

Then I was diagnosed with pancreatic cancer and told I had only a few weeks or perhaps months to live. Oy vey, no time for procrastination!

A few months prior to my diagnosis, when I first met my editor and writing coach, Stacey Stern, she asked me what I hoped to accomplish through writing my book and, more broadly, what I wanted to experience in my life. I told her I wanted to do two things before I died. One, make a contribution to the world by creating something that would have a healing impact on others, and two, fall in love. At the time we laughed when she said that although she couldn't make any promises about the falling in love piece, she absolutely could help me with my first goal.

After my diagnosis, the deadline was upon us. Literally. How *had* I evolved? How had I healed? Were there turning points? Fortunately, I had kept journals and written stories and poems over the years. As I read through them, I thought, *Oh my God, I have changed a lot. I was really depressed back then.*

But through all my down times, I never gave up. I persevered through therapy and one anti-depressant after another—in fact, I switched anti-depressants *thirty-four* times before I found the one that consistently worked well for me. I pressed ahead with constant questioning and a multitude of healers until I ultimately learned how to have compassion for myself. Every journal page I read made me proud of the work I've done and the person I've become.

In a way that I never could have anticipated, I accomplished my second goal. While I didn't fall in love with another person, and for that there is a sense of disappointment, I have learned to love myself deeply. I know I am a beautiful person, and I no longer blame myself for the pain I have experienced.

I am at peace with dying. It has been a long road, and I am tired. But more than that, I believe I have done what I came here to do. I overcame what I needed to, and now it is time to move on.

Note from the Coauthor

To say that Eliana rose to the challenge of giving everything to this book during her final weeks would be an understatement. When Eliana called me on October 29, 2018, with the shocking news of her terminal cancer—and the more stunning news of how little time she likely had left—I thought she was saying goodbye. She wasn't.

Eliana was more determined than ever to look deep within and mine the lessons of her life. We discussed at length how to proceed with her memoir in a way that was authentically Eliana, without sugarcoating or oversimplifying the complex being and tenacious spiritual seeker she was. Although Eliana wrestled mightily with depression beginning at a young age, she had been in a better, more contented place for the past ten years. Still, she was the first to say she was not an expert on overcoming depression, and we agreed this wouldn't be a how-to book on the subject. That wasn't her style.

Eliana was a gifted artist, prolific in many mediums. When she invited me into her home and generously turned over her entire bookshelf of journals filled with her innermost thoughts, I discovered raw, honest poetry and short stories of her adventures. I also encountered imagined conversations with God, self-inquiries in her search for purpose and meaning, and vignettes she wrote in the third person about herself.

Her eclectic writing collection, combined with the many hours we spent talking at her bedside and in her living room as her death approached, provided ample material for an illuminating albeit untraditional act three. We agreed that given the circumstances, the purest way to present the truth of her life and capture her peace about dying required that we go beyond a continually uniform narrative. This is why act three is presented in a style utterly unlike the first two acts. Eliana marched to the beat of her own drum until the very end. Thank you in advance for forgiving our departure from convention.

May Eliana's openhearted memoir shed light on your own troubles or those of your loved ones, and may you be blessed by her offering.

Prologue

If you were born before 1965, you probably remember the Moonies. During the 1970s and early '80s they were the biggest cult around. If you spent any time around San Francisco back then, while you were hanging out at Fisherman's Wharf or ambling across the Berkeley campus, a Moonie may even have cozied up to you and invited you to dinner. And that Moonie may have been me.

The official name of the Moonies was the Unification Church. The group was dubbed the Moonies (some would say pejoratively) based on the name of the church's founder and leader, Reverend Sun Myung Moon. Moon was from Korea, where he started the church in the 1950s. He moved to the United States in 1971, and by the end of that decade, there were roughly five thousand Moonies in America, most of them in their early twenties.

I dropped out of college and joined the church in 1975 at the age of twenty-one, and I stayed for six years. Young and idealistic, my fellow Moonies and I believed we could save the world and reestablish God's Kingdom here on Earth by following Reverend Moon. This conviction motivated us to work long hours, sleep very little, and give all our earnings to the church. Reverend Moon lived in a mansion, while we slept on the floor. He proclaimed he was the Messiah. We believed him.

Some people said we were brainwashed. Others said we were under mind control. I believe everyone is under mind control to some degree. Our families, peer groups, religious affiliations, and even the sources we turn to for our news mold our thinking, shape our worldview, and secure us with blinders so we can't see life clearly from other perspectives.

But the Moonies pushed this further. We lived together, worked together, and had tight restrictions on whom we could talk to and what we could read. We were deprived of sleep and had no time for self-reflection. Even so, we were convinced that *we* had taken off our blinders while the rest of the world continued to wear theirs.

To this day, I am tempted to dismiss those who say we were brainwashed. Not because there isn't some truth to it, but because it implies that we lost our unique personalities and became automatons. I get defensive about that because it's not the whole truth.

Before joining the church, I had been searching earnestly for purpose and meaning in my life, and initially the Moonies seemed to be the answer to my prayers. My first month on their farm in Boonville, California, was glorious. Along with dozens of other passionate idealists, I was going to save the world while living on six hundred beautiful acres in Northern California, singing, picking apples, cooking meals, and romping through the mud. What could be better than that?

I was hooked. Not only had I found a wonderful group of people to live with, but for the first time in my life, I also experienced an exquisite love affair with God. That was the clincher.

But my Boonville honeymoon didn't last. I was sent down to San Francisco to live in one of our communal houses, where life was not nearly as carefree. I spent the next six years either recruiting people to join the church or selling flowers to raise money for the church.

My time in the Moonies was empowering, adventurous, and deeply spiritual—except when it was disempowering, mind numbing, and disorienting. I was a shy introvert when I joined, and with gritty determination, I burst from my shell. I creatively turned mundane routines and grueling days into gutsy adventures. While I forfeited individual choice in many areas of my life—and here's the rub—I also felt tremendously empowered to cultivate parts of myself that previously had been hidden or neglected.

I felt alive and loved by God. I was often proud of myself and believed I was becoming a stronger, better, more confident version of me. But there were also times I felt conflicted and confused. There were long stretches when my connection to God felt like a distant memory, while at other times we were constant companions. The most compelling, delicious moments were when I felt profoundly seen, accepted, and loved by God.

When I was ripped from the church by the kidnappers and deprogrammers my parents hired, everything changed. I retreated into myself. I felt awkward around people, including my family. When I returned to college, it took me six months before I was ready to interact with my peers. I was dumbstruck. I thought God had abandoned me. My life felt meaningless. What happened to the woman who had blossomed and reveled in bold adventures? How could I ever trust myself again when I had been bamboozled by a story that wasn't true?

For the next three to four decades, I put my Moonie experience in a box and ached over my lost connection to the Divine. My speculation about the existence and nature of God evolved over the years, but I held fast to my story that I had a special connection to God while I was a Moonie and that it had never been the same since then.

Then, during a creative writing and art class in 2017, the teacher posed a series of soulful questions to contemplate. *When was your first encounter with the Divine? What has been your most profound experience in life?* Questions of that nature.

As I wrote out my answers, I noticed I was defaulting to my longstanding storyline that all my deepest experiences occurred while I was in the church and that my internal spiritual landscape had subsequently been comparatively dry.

But was this really true? I was finally ready to reconsider the stories I had been telling myself and others about my years as a Moonie and my relationship with the Divine. It was time to revisit the draft manuscript I had begun fifteen years earlier and to actually finish my book.

Whether or not you've had any experience with a cult or know people who have, I hope my story will resonate with you. Although it has been more than forty years since I first joined the Unification Church, I remember some events with exquisite clarity (or at least I think I do), while others are fuzzy. I am very grateful that my parents saved fifty of the letters I wrote to them during those years, which greatly aided in refreshing certain memories.

When I couldn't remember precisely what someone said or what they looked like, and if I didn't have letters to jog my memory, I have taken the liberty to make up details and fill in gaps. To the best of my ability, I have portrayed the truthful essence of whatever was going on—at least, how I saw it from my inherently subjective perspective.

A bit more about names. With the exception of my family and my pets, I have changed the names of others to protect their privacy. My own name changes in this book as well. My given name at birth was Ellen, and that is how I refer to myself throughout the first two acts. Since I legally changed my name to Eliana years after I left the Moonies, I refer to myself as Eliana in much of the third act.

Act One

Searching for Purpose
(1960s–1970s)

1

Dinner with Destiny

Already world-weary at the age of twenty-one, I flopped down on the lawn of the Santa Rosa Junior College campus in September 1975 and kicked off my sandals. The grass was prickly on my outstretched arms and legs, and the sun soaked into my face. As I closed my eyes to savor the warmth, I imagined my body sinking into the earth, sinking so deep that I merged with it. I imagined I was dying.

But this was not the time to obsess about death. No, I had to make phone calls to find a place to rent. I was staying with people I barely knew, and I had to be out by Friday—just two days away.

I forced myself back up and crossed the field where shirtless boys with golden-brown chests and six-pack abs were playing Frisbee. Whooping and hollering. Where did they get the energy? Several women were gathered on the stone steps eating lunch out of brown paper bags, while nearby a boy hunched over his guitar quietly singing Simon and Garfunkel's "Bridge Over Troubled Water."

The first day of class was the next day, and going back to school had been a last-minute decision. I had hoped something better would come up, but since it hadn't and Santa Rosa Junior College was just down the road from where I'd been living in Sebastopol, I signed up for courses in painting and costume design. This was my second attempt at college. I had dropped out of Fairhaven College in Bellingham, Washington, the previous year with high hopes of taking a year to explore and discover my true path, but that plan hadn't quite come together.

Sunlight streamed through the glass doors of the student union, creating a sharp diagonal line between the shadow and the light. Tucked against the wall on the darker side of the room, the pay phone was enclosed in a tall glass box with a waffle door. One woman was standing in line for the phone, and I took my place behind her.

My purse, made from textured yarn in rich ruby tones, hung from my shoulder. I scrounged around inside it and pulled out my small green spiral notebook. It was filled with the phone numbers for potential places to live, and most of the entries were crossed out. Why couldn't I find a home where people ate dinner together? Was that too much to ask?

When I met with prospective housemates, my first question was always, "Do you eat dinner together?" So far, no one said they did. It wasn't just that I wanted to eat dinner with my housemates, it was more that I wanted a home that felt cozy and friendly, and eating dinner together seemed like a good litmus test.

The woman in front of me was eating an orange. The smell reminded me of my mother. When we were kids, she made our lunch every morning before school. She'd line the previously used, crinkled brown paper bags up on the counter and write our names in blue felt pen: Kim, Jan, Ellen, and Judy. Before packing an orange, she'd cut a thin slice off the top and bottom, then score the sides to make it easy for us to peel.

"Are you a student here?"

Startled, I looked up at the woman in line in front of me. "Are you talking to me?"

She was wearing a white cotton long-sleeved blouse buttoned up to the throat and brown polyester pants. Most of the other female students were half naked in shorts and tank tops. I had on a pair of green shorts, a periwinkle-blue short-sleeved blouse, and my Dr. Scholl's sandals, the Birkenstocks of the '70s.

"Sorry if I scared you." She smiled a shy, self-conscious smile. "I just asked if you were a student here."

"Yeah, today's my first day," I replied. "How about you? Do you go here?"

"No, I'm just visiting." She paused, looking hesitant. "I um, I live with a community on a big farm in Mendocino County."

"That sounds cool." I stood with my arms crossed. Was this a conversation? Should I say something else?

"We also have several houses in the Bay Area," she continued. "We take the food we grow on the farm and give it away to poor people in Oakland."

"Is your group religious?"

"No, not really." Her pale skin flushed. "It's called Creative Community Project."

Her voice was soft and alluring. I had to lean in to hear her. She smelled like hay, which made me yearn for summer camp. I loved camp. I had spent a month for five consecutive summers at Camp Trinity in Northern California's Trinity Alps Wilderness. Singing under the apple trees, skinny-dipping in the river, and sleeping under the stars was Heaven on Earth for me.

Growing up in Los Angeles, I hated the fast pace, the smog, and the congestion of the city. I always imagined that someday I'd live in the woods or out in the country, far away from LA. In high school I had fantasies of building my own house, and everything in it would be handmade, either by me or by friends. One wall of my kitchen would be like a garage door, so when you opened it, it would feel like you were cooking outside.

The waffle door of the telephone booth opened, and a boy squeezed out.

"You can go next, I'm not in a hurry," the woman in front of me said.

"Are you sure?"

"Yeah, go ahead."

Inside the phone booth I tried to balance my notebook, pen, and wallet on the small shelf while dialing.

"Please deposit ten cents."

My wallet fell to the floor and change scattered.

"Shit."

I dropped the phone receiver and knelt down to pick up the change.

"Please deposit ten cents."

"Okay, okay, hold on," I called to the dangling phone.

After five calls to potential housemates, only one sounded promising. Two women, three acres, a few fruit trees, down a dirt road, and not too far from campus. But the woman I spoke with said I couldn't visit until Friday afternoon. If I didn't like this place, I was screwed.

When I stepped out of the phone booth, I noticed that the person who had been standing before me in line was now staring blankly at the flyers on the bulletin board, as if she wasn't really reading them. I sat down to make a few notes on my list, and she came over to me. She smiled awkwardly.

"I hope I'm not bothering you. I just wanted to let you know that our community is going to have an open house dinner on Friday night, and you're welcome to come."

Why was she inviting me to dinner? Perfect strangers don't usually invite you to dinner. Her community did sound pretty cool, but I didn't like parties. I was okay with talking to people one-on-one, but when I was in a group I tended to stumble over my words and turn red when I tried to speak up. Besides, I might be moving into my new place on Friday.

She handed me a Xeroxed purple piece of paper with the words "Creative Community Project" written in an arc like a rainbow across the top, with hand-drawn, smiling people holding hands below. She wrote the time and place to meet on the back and signed it *Lucy*. I accepted the piece of paper and told her I'd think about it, just to be polite, although I had no intention of going. I folded the paper and slid it into my purse.

On Friday afternoon I drove my Honda Civic hatchback down a dirt road on the edge of town to visit my prospective new home. Apple trees lined the road and the air smelled of fermented rotting apples. Dust smeared across my windshield. My gut was tense with hopeful anticipation that this house and these people would be a good fit—as well as anxious dread that they would not.

The road was less than a mile long, and at the end I pulled my car up to the front of a dark-red ranch house. The paint was weathered, though not in a bad way. It helped the house blend in with the untamed landscape. The screen door was ripped. Did that mean they had dogs or just hadn't bothered to fix it?

As I walked toward the house a woman came out to greet me.

"Hi, I'm Sharon," she called.

"Hi, I'm Ellen." My smile felt strained. At least she was friendly.

"Why don't you come around back into the yard." I followed her along the side of the house. "Would you like some lemonade?"

"Sure, that would be great." I coaxed myself to try to relax.

The yard was spacious with patchy brown grass and no flowers. A few chickens bobbed their heads and made squawking sounds as they pecked the ground. A small grove of lemon trees, heavy with lemons, seduced me with their fragrance. Chickens and lemon trees, a good start. Those made up for the neglect I saw throughout the rest of the yard.

I sat down at the redwood picnic table, and Sharon brought out two tall glasses of lemonade with ice.

"I made the lemonade from our own lemons."

Another promising sign. Maybe we could bake bread together with eggs from the chickens. I used to bake a lot, back in high school. My first job was baking quiche and cheesecake for a catering company. My sister Jan and I used to find the hardest dessert in the cookbook and try our skills at making it.

Beads of condensation ran down my glass of lemonade. I took a sip, and the cold liquid teased my taste buds with a punch of sour infused with sweet.

Sharon and I talked for half an hour. We might not become best friends, I thought, but I could see myself living there. As far as I could tell, I passed the test with her.

She shared the place with another woman, Ariel. Sharon told me that before it was a done deal, Ariel had to give her okay.

"I need to let you know that Ariel has some rules." Sharon's voice was hesitant, like she wasn't in total agreement with the rules.

"Ariel is a lesbian, and she doesn't want any men coming over to the house."

"What?" I was stunned. "Ever?" I paused and let my emotions reorganize themselves. "Even if she's not home?"

"Yeah, even if she's not home."

I took another sip of lemonade and winced at the sour taste—all the sugar had sunk to the bottom.

"I have to think about it," I told Sharon. Pushing the glass away, I got up and walked back to my car. Then I drove around the corner, pulled to the side of the road, cut the engine, and cried. What an asshole! Just because she didn't like men, she had to make the rest of us do whatever she wanted. Now, what the hell was I supposed to do?

I wailed for a few minutes, until most of the distress left my body. Shit. I guess I'll have to plead with Lisa to let me stay a few more days.

It was ten to six. What time was that dinner? I reached into my purse and pulled out the invitation. It said to meet in front of the college at 6:00 p.m. Inhaling deeply to collect myself, I figured I might as well go. What did I have to lose?

When I pulled into a No Parking zone a few minutes after six, I spotted Lucy standing next to a school bus, encouraging people to file on. I lifted my arms and smelled under each armpit, then used a paper towel to wipe the sweat away. They'd pass. I got out of my car and headed to Lucy. I was in that post-crying, washed-clean zone where no matter what happened, it would be fine.

"Do I still have time to go to your dinner? I have to park my car."

Lucy looked surprised. "Hey, you came. I really didn't think you would. I mean, it's great you're here. Yeah, go park your car. You can drive over to the park with me."

The park was about ten minutes from the school. We got out of the car, and I scanned the scene. Twenty or so people were sitting on logs around a firepit with a blazing fire, singing songs—folk songs and songs I sang at camp. Off to the side, a few people were cutting up vegetables and stirring huge pots of food.

Lucy led me to a seat on a log near the campfire. A good-looking guy with wavy brown hair sat on a stump, holding his guitar on his knee. "What should we sing next?" he asked the group.

"You Are My Sunshine," someone called out.

The group sang full gusto, while in a tentative voice, I joined in.

They seemed like such healthy, wholesome people. Where had they been hiding? Most people my age seemed too concerned about looking cool to sing sentimental camp songs. With each song, I breathed a little deeper and sang a little louder. This felt good. It felt real. I craved authenticity. I craved community. Dusk softened the sky.

After a few songs, a tall, wiry guy asked us to stand in a circle and hold hands.

"Hi, my name's Luke. Welcome to our family. We're so glad you could all come. Before we have dinner let's go around the circle and introduce ourselves."

Halfway around the circle a short girl with curly black hair spoke. "Hi, my name's Ann."

I couldn't believe it—I knew her. Not well, but one familiar face made this group of strangers feel a whole lot safer. I had met Ann at a party the previous spring, and then I'd given her a ride from Sebastopol to her mother's house in Los Angeles. I'd seen the house where she grew up, I'd met her mother, and they were Jewish—we were part of the same tribe, so she was almost family.

When we finished introducing ourselves, Ann ran across the circle and threw her arms around me. I hugged her back, though not quite as enthusiastically.

"I'm so glad you're here. This place is incredible. Who did you meet?"

I glanced at Lucy, who was standing next to me. "Lucy invited me, if that's what you mean."

"I guess you two know each other?" Lucy beamed with satisfaction.

"Oh yeah. We took a long ride to LA together. We had lots of time to get to know each other, right?" Ann smiled at me like we were long-lost friends. I nodded in return.

"Well, why don't you two talk while I go get dinner."

Ann led us back to the log where we'd been sitting before.

"How long have you been part of this group?" I asked her once we sat down.

"For two months. I met them in July, and I haven't left since. It's been so great. I live on the farm up in Mendocino."

Within me a barely audible voice whispered, "Maybe this is what you've been looking for."

Lucy returned and handed each of us a plate of spaghetti, garlic bread, and salad, then went to get her own plate.

"What do you do on the farm?"

"We're all in different groups, and each group has a different job. Sometimes I work in the garden, sometimes I cook, sometimes I chop wood."

I could see myself doing all of those things.

Lucy returned with her dinner and sat down beside me. Around us small groups of two or three people were eating and chatting. After everyone was served, Luke stood up and we all turned to focus on him. An expectant silence wove us together.

"Good evening, friends. I'd like to tell you a bit about our community." His boyish enthusiasm was charming.

"As many of you know, we have a six-hundred-acre farm up in Mendocino County and several houses in the Bay Area. But we're more than just a group of people living together. We want to build an ideal community. And not just for ourselves, but for the whole world. You may be thinking, 'Oh sure, that's impossible.' But we don't think it is, and we're committed to making it happen. So, let me tell you a little story to demonstrate our philosophy. Once upon a time there was a huge elephant."

A call for the elephant came from the edge of the circle, and an elephant ambled in, comprised of three people in contorted positions. The first person leaned forward, swinging his arms together, resembling an elephant's trunk. The second person bent over and held onto the waist of the first person, forming the middle of the elephant. The third person bent backwards, so that her ponytail hung down like a tail.

Luke continued. "There were also three wise men, who all happened to be blind."

Three people approached the elephant, stumbling around, scratching their pretend beards, furrowing their brows, and attempting to look wise.

"Now each wise man thought he knew the whole truth about elephants. The first wise man ..."

On cue, the first wise man stepped forward and approached the front of the elephant.

"Even though I'm blind, I can tell you exactly what an elephant looks like."

He felt the elephant's trunk.

"An elephant is long and narrow, like two arms," he said.

"No, no, no," exclaimed the second wise man. Now he walked forward and touched the middle of the elephant. "An elephant is not like two arms. What are you talking about? Can't you feel anything? It's like ..." He paused pensively, "like a human torso. An elephant is like a human torso. That's what it is."

"Are you crazy?" the third wise man cried. He moved forward and touched the elephant's tail. "This feels nothing like a human torso. It's like a pony's tail. An elephant is exactly like a pony's tail."

The three wise men barked at each other.

"An elephant is like two arms!"

"No, an elephant is like a torso!"

"No, an elephant is like a pony's tail!"

Luke interrupted. "Elephant, wise men, be gone." The elephant hobbled off the makeshift stage with the squabbling wise men trailing behind.

"We can recognize the problem because we have the perspective to see that an elephant isn't just one of these things, it's all of them. The wise men argued because they each had a limited point of view. But when you can see the whole truth, you understand how all the smaller truths fit together. That's what we're trying to do in our community— discover the whole truth about life so we can live more satisfying, harmonious lives together."

Everyone clapped, and all of the characters took a bow. Luke continued, "We hope you enjoyed the evening and that you will join us on our adventure. If you're interested in coming to our retreat this weekend, please talk to the person who brought you tonight. Thank you."

This felt like camp with a purpose. What an ideal combination. Ann had gone to help clean up. I looked at Lucy. "What retreat?" I asked.

"We're having a special retreat this weekend up on our farm, which is about ninety minutes from here, in a little town called Boonville. Do you think you could come?"

"Well, since I didn't know anything about it until this minute, probably not. Maybe next time."

"We don't have the retreat every weekend, and this is going to include special workshops. I wouldn't want you to miss it."

"I'm interested, but I don't have any other clothes with me. And I have homework to do. School just started, and I don't want to get behind right from the beginning."

"Don't worry about that. What you're wearing is just fine, and I can loan you a sweater and a sleeping bag."

"You could? But what about my homework? Do you think there'd be time to do my homework?"

"Oh, sure, we could make time."

"Well, okay." I paused. "Oh, how much does it cost?" In my excitement I hadn't even considered cost. Now I was waiting for her to let me down.

"Eighteen dollars." She seemed nervous that I'd balk at the price. "That's for two days and all your meals."

"That's it? I can afford that." After all, last year I had paid two hundred dollars for the est training, a popular personal growth workshop. And that didn't include food or lodging.

I checked inside myself and asked my higher self if I wanted to go. The answer was a resounding *Yes!*

"I'll do it."

Lucy beamed. "Great."

By the time we finished talking, almost everyone else had gone. I was so caught up talking to Lucy about the retreat that I hadn't noticed the others leaving.

"The bus has already taken off," Lucy said, "so we'll drive up with Jay."

All three of us piled into the front of Jay's pickup. Leaning my head on the window, I quickly fell asleep. An hour and a half later, around midnight, Lucy gently nudged me.

"I have to get out to open the gate," she whispered.

The moment I stepped out of the truck to let Lucy out, I swooned at the smell of damp hay and fresh air. I paused and whispered silent words of gratitude. Lucy jumped out of the truck, and I climbed back in. We drove through the gate, Lucy got back in, and we slowly bounced down the dirt road to the parking lot.

Jay parked the car, then, shining his flashlight in front of us, he guided us down a path, across a small bridge, and up a trail to an open, grassy area softly illuminated by a few lights. Everything was quiet. "Goodnight," he said. "Sleep well. See you in the morning."

I saw a few structures but couldn't make out what they were.

"That's the Green Trailer where the sisters sleep," Lucy said as she pointed to the building next to us. "The brothers sleep in the building over there, behind the trailer."

I had gone to a college with coed dorms. In this age of "free love," it was refreshing to know that here the men and women slept separately. By the way, when did we become men and women rather than boys and girls? I personally felt like I was teetering on the edge between childhood and adulthood, and I liked the sound of brothers and sisters.

"Those are the brothers' bathrooms, and those are the sisters'," Lucy said as she pointed to sheds off to the left. "Do you need to use the bathroom before going to bed?"

"Yeah."

"Okay, I'll meet you back here. I'm going to get you a sleeping bag and a T-shirt to sleep in."

When Lucy walked away, I stretched out my arms, smiled up at the brilliant stars, and hugged the intoxicating country air.

The bathroom was a three-sided wooden structure with a tin roof. There were two sinks on the front porch, and beyond the sinks were two enclosed stalls with toilets. I found a tube of toothpaste on the sink and squeezed some onto my finger to brush my teeth.

Afterward, Lucy guided me to the front door of the Green Trailer. "Everyone's probably sleeping, so be quiet when you go in. It might be hard to find a place to sleep—just lay your bag down anywhere you can find space."

When she opened the door, I saw sleeping bags spread out all over the floor. Tiptoeing among the sleeping women, I found a space on the floor just wide enough to squeeze into. I unrolled my bag, changed into Lucy's T-shirt, made a pillow out of my bunched-up clothes, then snuggled deep inside the sleeping bag with the red plaid flannel lining soft against my skin.

"Thank you," I whispered, and quickly fell asleep.

2

Too Good to Be True

A few hours later, the morning sun peeked through the narrow, east-facing windows of the Green Trailer.

"When the red, red robin comes bob bob bobbin' along, along …"

Startled awake, I opened my eyes and saw three women standing just inside the door of the trailer. One strummed her guitar and all three sang with enthusiastic animation, as if to a kindergarten class.

"There'll be no more sobbin' when he starts singing his old, sweet song …"

Women were sitting up, yawning, and crawling out of their sleeping bags. Some even jumped up in the air and whispered something to themselves. Most of the walls that normally divide a trailer into rooms had been removed, so this was just one long room filled to the brim with fifty waking women.

"Wake up, wake up, you sleepyheads. Get up, get out of bed. Cheer up, cheer up, the sun is red. Live, love, laugh, and be happy ..."

"Good morning, sisters!" called the one with the guitar. "Welcome to Boonville. Exercises at 8:00 a.m."

As they walked out, I could still hear the guitar lady strumming as they passed by the trailer window.

Ann spotted me and jumped over several bodies to greet me. "Good morning. I'm so glad you made it up here. Can I help you with anything?"

"No, I'm fine." I yawned. "Where's Lucy?"

"She has some other things to do, so I'm going to take care of you this weekend."

I put my clothes back on and rolled up my sleeping bag. "Where should I put this? Lucy loaned it to me."

Ann showed me where all of the sleeping bags were rolled and stored.

"I'm going to the bathroom," I told her.

"I'll go with you. Lucy gave me this for you." It was a toothbrush.

"Oh, thank you. You've made my day."

We went outside to the bathroom. Several women were at each sink, washing their faces and brushing their teeth. We waited in line. Around me people were greeting each other with smiles and hugs.

"When you're done, wait here for me," Ann told me.

While waiting for Ann after I finished in the bathroom, several people greeted me. "Hi, what's your name? Is this your first weekend? I hope you enjoy yourself."

From what Lucy had told me, I thought this was a special, infrequently held retreat. But people kept asking me, "Is
this your first weekend?"

Ann came and took me by the arm. I let her hold it for a
few minutes just to be gracious, then casually withdrew it.

"What's that?" I asked, pointing to a large, dilapidated
barn with cracks between the boards.

"That's the Chicken Palace. It's where the boys sleep and
where we have lectures."

Lectures? I hadn't planned on lectures.

"And we just call this the Green Trailer, where we slept
last night." We started walking in the direction everyone else
was going. "And that's the White Trailer. That's where the
kitchen is and where the staff sleeps."

The White Trailer was about the same size as the green
one. It hardly looked large enough for a kitchen plus staff
bedrooms. About a hundred people stood in a circle in the
field in front of the White Trailer. One woman stood in the
middle, leading exercises—some yoga and calisthenics. After
about twenty minutes, a small group of people came out of
the White Trailer and joined the circle. The woman who had
played guitar that morning was one of them. She spoke first.

"Good morning, brothers and sisters. My name is Susie.
Let's sing one more song before we split up into our groups
and have breakfast. Jake and Lynn, would you hand out the
songbooks?"

Susie, who looked like she was in her mid-twenties, wore
her long brown hair pulled back into a ponytail, a flowered
skirt to her knees, and a white tailored blouse. A pile of paper

songbooks with bright-blue covers was stacked in the center of the circle. A young man and woman gathered them up and handed them to every other person.

"Let's sing 'There's a Place for Us.' You can find it on page twenty-seven."

"There's a place for us, Somewhere a place for us. Peace and quiet and open air ... Hold my hand and I'll take you there ..."

We all held hands and swayed as we sang. But the people to my left swayed one direction while the people to my right swayed the other, pulling and crashing where I joined them together.

When we finished the song, a man stepped forward. He was about five feet eight, a little pudgy, and he looked Jewish. Although I can't list the characteristics someone needs to possess to look Jewish—and this may sound odd to the un-initiated—picking out fellow members of our tribe is a game we Jews sometimes play. It's a bonding thing that can facili-tate connection with a new acquaintance.

"Welcome, brothers and sisters. My name is Daniel." Everyone stood still, and I released the hands of the people next to me. "I want to offer a prayer." He closed his eyes. "Heavenly Father, thank you so much for this beautiful day. Thank you for the brothers and sisters gathered here. We're so grateful to be part of this family. Please bless the food we're about to eat."

Heavenly Father? Lucy told me this place wasn't reli-gious. Worse than that, Heavenly Father sounded Christian, and I certainly didn't want to be part of a Christian group.

Daniel spoke again. "We're going to divide up into groups, and the people in your group will be your family for the weekend. First, I'll call a group leader's name. When I call your name, go stand by your group leader."

Dina, my group leader, wore a short scarf around her neck. She looked spunky and natural. Lucy was her assistant. Ann was also in our group, along with five others. After we assembled, Lucy asked one of the others to get the breakfast while we found a place to eat. As we walked up the side of a hill, Dina walked beside me.

"I hear Lucy met you in Santa Rosa."

The tone of her voice and the brush of her arm against mine felt so intimate, I let my fears of this being a "God group" recede into the background.

One of the group members spread out a blanket under a tree.

"Here, Ellen, sit next to me." Dina patted the blanket beside her, and I basked in the pleasure of being chosen. We sat in a circle, with Ann seated on my other side.

"Let's do a choo-choo pow. For those of you who don't know what this is, just hold on," directed Dina, the dimple in her cheek further drawing me in.

Everyone held hands. A few blank faces amid eager smiles. They must be new too, I thought. "Choo-choo-choo, choo-choo-choo, choo-choo-choo, yeah, yeah, pow!" cried everyone else. Those who knew what they were doing vigorously raised and lowered their hands along with their neighbors' hands, in sync with the chant. I felt jostled but smiled back at the hopeful crowd.

"While we're waiting for breakfast, let's go around the circle and say our name, who brought us here, and how long we've been here. Lucy, do you want to start?"

"My name's Lucy. I first met Sally two years ago, and I've been here ever since."

She spoke so softly that I had to strain to hear her. I wanted to growl, "Would you please talk louder?" I got irritated easily.

The guy with breakfast stood outside the circle, waiting for Lucy to finish. When she was done speaking, he slipped into the circle and placed a cardboard box in the middle. Lucy helped him take little cardboard bowls of granola out of the box and pass them around. Then they passed around oranges, plastic spoons, napkins, and a pitcher of milk.

Starving, I poured milk on my cereal. The milk was disappointingly watery. It was probably that powdered stuff. I much preferred whole milk. A few years ago, when I lived in a house on a lake with five other people, we got milk straight from a farm in gallon-sized glass jars. I'd scoop the cream off the top to pour over my cereal. But here, in the name of this new adventure, I let my distaste for powdered milk go.

We went around the circle introducing ourselves. Only one other person was there for the first time. The others had been part of the group anywhere from two weeks to three years. Each person had a story to tell. One after the other, they talked about how they'd been searching for meaning in their lives. They'd tried yoga, meditation, politics, graduate school. But something was always missing. Until now. After years of searching, they finally found the answer.

"This is our little family for the weekend," Dina explained. "We'll stick together throughout all of the activities. If you have questions, needs, or concerns at any time, ask the person who brought you. We have a very full weekend, so make sure you get enough sleep and enough to eat."

When Jack, the guy sitting on the other side of Dina, finished his granola, Dina wordlessly scooted her bowl over to him so he could have more. "Here's the schedule for today," she continued. "Right after breakfast we'll have a lecture, then we'll reconvene in our group for lunch. After lunch we'll play dodgeball, have a snack, and go back for another lecture. After the lecture, we'll have dinner. During dinner we'll write a song for the evening entertainment. Then the whole camp will gather together to sing the songs we've written for each other."

Lucy checked her watch, touched Dina on the arm, and quietly said, "Time to go."

"Okay everyone, meet in the Chicken Palace in ten minutes. We'll sit together for the lecture. Jack, will you clean up?"

I stood up and headed down the hill. "Wait for me," called Ann.

"I'm going to the bathroom."

"I'll come with you."

I wanted to walk alone or maybe with Lucy or Dina, but I waited for Ann to catch up with me. Inside the Chicken Palace, rows of folding chairs faced a small stage that was raised about a foot above the rest of the floor. A drum set, speakers, and microphones crowded the stage. Other than the stage and instruments, the Chicken Palace looked as much like a barn on the inside as it did on the outside. One large rectangular room with bare, weathered walls, a wooden floor, and three oversize doors. Ann and I found two seats in the third row next to the rest of our group, as people from other groups continued to stream in the doors.

Watching the people around me, I tried to categorize them but was struck by their diverse attire. Some men had scraggly beards and long hair, while others were clean-cut and wore polyester pants. Some women wore flowing hippie skirts or patches on their worn jeans, while others donned knee-length skirts and blouses buttoned puritanically close around the neck.

A band of four took their places on the stage. The guy who'd played guitar at the campfire the night before was on drums. Another guy was on fiddle, a woman played the clarinet, and Daniel was at the microphone.

"One, two, three, four ..."

"I pulled into Nazareth, was feeling 'bout half past dead. I just need some place, where I can lay my head. 'Hey, mister, can you tell me, where a man might find a bed?'"

The band wailed as the audience sang along. Some of the songs were familiar and some had a religious theme. The religious ones often had a fighting spirit, with lyrics about being soldiers for God. With each song the excitement rose until nearly everyone was standing and clapping in unison. Ann nudged me to join in with the same gusto that the others displayed. Still tentative, I stood, clapped, and sang, but I lacked the fervor of those around me. I wasn't ready to throw myself in with unbridled enthusiasm.

The band was a confusing mixture of rock-band exuberance in white-collar attire. The men wore dark polyester pants and white button-down shirts, and the woman wore a long plaid skirt and white blouse. It was odd. When they finished their set, Daniel wiped the sweat dripping down his forehead and embraced the audience with his impish smile. Earlier that morning his serious countenance intimidated me, but now his sweet face and round body evoked the Pillsbury doughboy. I couldn't be intimidated by the Pillsbury doughboy.

"Thank you, brothers and sisters! We have a very special treat for you all. Catherine, one of the founders of our community, is going to tell us about the ideal world. Everyone, please welcome Catherine."

Two people moved the podium to the middle of the stage, and a young woman placed a flower in a glass on the podium. The audience sat back down as Catherine took the stage with imposing self-confidence, her hair in a French roll and a colorful scarf flung around her neck.

"We speak of love and happiness here. That's the purpose of this weekend. But to receive love and happiness, you have to open yourselves up. It can be scary. Each one of you is like a seed. On its own, a seed doesn't look like much, but in the right environment, it can grow into a tree. You, too, are packed with creative potential. All you need is the right environment and the right nutrients to grow.

"This weekend is a great opportunity to open up and receive all the nutrients you need to manifest your creative potential. You need to give one hundred percent if you want to receive one hundred percent. You have so much potential.

"We are not studying from one point of view; rather, we are studying from the largest perspective. It takes tremendous open-mindedness to know truth. When we are able to understand ourselves from a whole perspective, we discover better ways to live.

"Some people like to say that truth is relative because it gives them permission to do whatever they want. But truth isn't relative. To find truth and actualize it begins by following conscientious common sense. A natural person is one who lives by conscientious common sense.

"If you are a natural person, you are at home anywhere in the cosmos—you can relate to everything. You don't have to be a different person for each occasion. Our desire for this weekend is to put conscientious common sense to work. We are not interested in theories of happiness; we want to *be* happy!"

Everyone around me cheered.

Catherine proceeded to describe why the world is the way it is. "In the beginning the world was perfect, but we were separated from God and lost our way. We need a guiding principle in order to know the right way to live."

She explained how each one of us needed to become a new kind of person and that an ideal community is based on maximizing our creative potential and loving and serving others. Each time Catherine mentioned God, I clenched. But then she'd assure us that we didn't have to use the word God. We could use the Universal Source of Love or anything else that felt good. We didn't have to believe in God to stay there.

She spoke for over an hour. Some people sat in rapt attention, while I noticed that a few others nodded off. I didn't know who belonged to this group versus who was a visitor like me, so I didn't know if those who dozed were members or visitors. When Catherine finished, everyone clapped and cheered before bustling out of the Chicken Palace.

Ann followed me to the bathroom again. "Wasn't that great?" she asked.

I was excited and inspired by the lecture, but why did Ann have to follow me everywhere? I would have preferred to wander off on my own, lie under a tree, and contemplate Catherine's words. Could these people really bring the world back into wholeness? Was that possible? I would do anything to be part of that.

That evening all the groups gathered in clusters in the Chicken Palace. Sitting on a blanket on the wood plank floor with paper plates overflowing with lasagna, cornbread, salad, and broccoli, we huddled around Dina.

"For those of you who are new, this will be a night of incredible entertainment. Each group is going to write a song, and we'll perform it later for all the other groups. Let your creativity flow, and let's come up with something great!"

Lucy was ready with paper and pen to write down suggestions.

"We need to choose a tune from a well-known song, then we'll make up our own words."

For the next hour we brainstormed tunes and words. At the end of the hour, we had written a song to the tune of John Denver's "Almost Heaven." I was impressed.

The people here had so much of what I was looking for. They were playful and purposeful. This community worked well together on a beautiful piece of land.

Over the next two hours, each group performed their song. Some sounded professionally polished, and some sounded amateurishly dorky. But either way, they cracked right through my defensive, judgmental veneer, and I felt surges of joy and camaraderie. Singing together can dissolve barriers and build bonds.

I had experienced this before—at concerts and protest marches where I felt closer to the strangers around me when we sang together. Here in the Chicken Palace, while singing songs we wrote ourselves about themes that glorified Boonville life, I felt a double wallop of intimacy and bonding.

At the conclusion of the evening program, we gathered for a group hug. Totally exhausted, I stumbled to bed. Snuggled in my sleeping bag, I looked around the room at the other fifty women who were squished together from wall to wall. At home I treasured my privacy, personal space, and time alone. But where had that gotten me? Catherine talked about building an ideal world. What was more important than that? But on the other hand, could I handle living in such close quarters for more than a weekend?

The next day began the same as the first. We woke up to the red robin song, exercised, met in our groups for breakfast, then filed into the Chicken Palace. The same bandmembers were on stage, but the tone was different today. People were quiet and subdued, and when the band played, the songs were tinged with sadness and longing.

After the band played a few songs, Catherine entered the stage. "Today we're going to find out why the world is not the way God originally planned it to be."

I sat attentive on the hard, folding chair. Even though I questioned whether or not there was a God, I had always wondered why the world was so messed up. It didn't make any sense. Why did people kill each other in wars instead of working out their differences with words? Even little kids are taught to use their words instead of hitting someone. Why were some people so poor and others so rich? With plenty of food in the world, why were some people still starving?

Catherine continued. "Jesus came in the position of the Messiah. He came to save the world. But the world didn't accept him, and so he did not accomplish his mission."

Wait a minute, what's with the Jesus stuff? I was on full alert. Lucy said this place wasn't religious. For me, anything to do with Jesus was off the table. Although I didn't celebrate many Jewish holidays or regularly attend temple, I was proud to be Jewish. It was a fundamental part of my identity, and I had no intention of messing with it.

Catherine continued with her story of how Jesus was betrayed and things did not go as God intended. The job of the Messiah is to create an ideal world, but that did not happen while Jesus was alive, nor had it happened since his death. As she finished her lecture, people all around me were crying. Some were sobbing while others were more muted.

I was distraught. Not because of her story, but because "Jesus" was interfering with my growing attachment to this group. Noticing my distress, Lucy took me to a quiet spot behind the Chicken Palace while the rest of the group met as usual.

I told her I didn't know anything about Christianity. I didn't know what Christians believed or what the New Testament said, but I knew I didn't want to be Christian. I was Jewish, and I couldn't be part of a group that was about Jesus.

In her soothing tone, Lucy addressed my fears. "The way we view Jesus is very different from traditional Christianity. We're not Christians, and you don't have to give up being Jewish to believe in what we're doing here. As a matter of fact, there are a lot of Jews here."

Knowing there were other Jews, including many in leadership positions, calmed my apprehensions. There was so much about this group I wanted to believe in, so I allowed Lucy's assurance that this was not a Christian group settle me.

The day continued with more lectures, eating, and singing. This group was going to build an ideal world. The lectures explained it, even if the process was kind of vague. Yet I could see they were putting it into practice right here on this beautiful farm. Everyone here was generous, playful, sincere, and loving.

This felt so right. Almost too good to be true. Isn't this exactly what I'd been looking for? I wouldn't mind dropping out of school. I had signed up for classes only because I hadn't come up with a better plan. Could this be it? Could I share my toothpaste with fifty other women, bump into each other as we spat in the sink, sleep on the floor night after night, have powdered milk on my granola? Could I do it? Would they want me? No one had invited me to stay.

On Sunday evening Catherine shared her story of how she joined The Family, which is how they referred to themselves. Her words penetrated my heart. I knew this is where I wanted to be. Afterward, Lucy and Dina took me down by the creek.

"Ellen, you are such a special sister. We would love it if you would stay here and help us build the Heavenly Kingdom."

They didn't have to push. My desire to do something meaningful was stronger than my desire for comfort and privacy. "Yes, I'd love to stay!"

3

Lost and Lonely

Before I get into what happened after I said yes to the Moonies—and by the way, at the time I had no idea what I had agreed to, much less that it was a cult known as the Moonies—I want to step back and tell you who I was before that fateful day.

The year is 1969. I'm sitting on my bed, simmering with anger. Why was I so angry? I didn't know. I couldn't point to anything specific. My mother said I was going through a stage because I was fifteen, and that's what teenagers did. But I argued that this wasn't a stage. Labeling it that minimized my very real feelings. Maybe I was angry with myself because I couldn't get myself to move off the bed and do something.

My watch lay on my nightstand, ticking, ticking madly away. Each tick reminded me that I was wasting time, wasting my life. I wanted to throw the watch across the room, but that wasn't my style. I wasn't impulsive like that.

Suddenly, I saw my hand grab the watch and sling the damn thing against the wall! I arched my eyebrows in surprise and cracked a wry smile—grateful and triumphant that some of my old feisty self was still here. She may be stuffed down, but she momentarily broke through this stuck place with spunky action.

Inside me were big, important thoughts, but I felt like I only knew how to express the inconsequential ones. The deeper ones were twisted together and jumbled up. I wished I had someone to talk to. Maybe I could untangle my thoughts if I only had someone to talk to. I missed Lisa. We had been best friends, but then we grew apart. I didn't know if she even liked me anymore. Why should she? I didn't feel like myself when I was with her. But then again, for the past few years, I didn't even feel like myself when I was by myself.

Two years earlier, I had a huge crush on my religious schoolteacher, Jonathan. My family belonged to a Jewish Reform Synagogue. For those unfamiliar with the denominations of Judaism, at that time, there were basically three. Reform Judaism was generally considered to be the most liberal, least religious, and most assimilated expression of Judaism. Conservative Judaism was more adherent to Jewish laws and traditions, and Orthodox Judaism was the strictest and most observant.

When our religious school class studied Jewish ethics and values, Jonathan made the stories from our textbooks come alive. He was able to inspire a class of thirteen-year-olds to express our innermost thoughts and feelings. It was novel to be with a group of my peers and talk authentically about how we felt. Actually, it was novel for me to talk honestly with *anyone* about my deepest thoughts and feelings.

I was introverted and shy, so while I didn't talk a lot in class, it impacted me greatly. And the way that Jonathan sincerely listened to each person gave me hope that someday I would be truly seen and understood. I craved that more than anything, so I developed an intense crush on him.

It's not that my parents—at least my mom—were unavailable for conversation. When I was younger, I shared a room with my little sister Judy, and every night my mother would come in to say good night to us. She'd sit on Judy's bed, and Judy would go on and on about all the details of her day, while my mother calmly listened. Judy thought we had the most nurturing mother in the world.

Then my mother would come sit on my bed. When she'd ask me about my day, I'd typically say, "It was fine." That was it. Not because I didn't have more to say but because that's all I seemed able to express. My mother was reserved, and I needed someone to draw me out. The combination didn't work in our favor.

Judy and I were close when we were young, but at fifteen, I shut her out along with everyone else. I even stopped whispering secrets to my cat, Cocoa, and locked my bedroom door so that Cocoa could no longer sleep with me (not that she could open the door if it wasn't locked). My oldest sister, Kim, had moved out to go to college by then, so I moved into her room.

I had been depressed before, but now it was all-encompassing. Although I acted like I didn't want to talk to anyone, I desperately longed for connection. When I tried to imagine who might "get" me, only Jonathan came to mind.

I heard he was working at a large bookstore in Westwood Village, a charming shopping area serving UCLA and the surrounding affluent neighborhoods. The village was a few miles from my house, so I rode my bike there and locked it outside the bookstore. With a pounding heart, I went in and asked if Jonathan was there.

Jonathan, clearly surprised to see me, greeted me with a warm hug. He asked how I was and if he could help me find a book, or was this a social call? With hesitation I asked if I could talk to him privately. We went into the basement of the bookstore where no one would disturb us.

"What do you want to talk about?"

I didn't know what to say. Inside, my feelings banged against each other, clamoring to come out, but I didn't know how to articulate them. We sat in silence. He encouraged me to say something, anything, but my feelings were a chaotic jumble, and they wouldn't assemble themselves into words. We sat with each other for about a half hour, and then Jonathan apologized, he had to get back to work.

Around this time I also decided to become a vegetarian. To be honest, it wasn't for principled reasons. I told others it was because I didn't want to kill animals (sometimes I even believed that), but the real impetus was that my former best friend Lisa was a vegetarian.

Lisa was passionate, she knew what she liked, and she was creative, always making things. I was jealous of those qualities. When I compared my room to hers, hers seemed like it was bustling with life—baskets overflowing with yarn, colored pencils on her desk, and her flute lying next to her guitar on the floor. I thought my room appeared stagnant, with everything in its proper place.

Although when I look back on it now, my room probably didn't look plain or boring to others. We lived in an old Spanish-style house, and my room had a curved fireplace with red Mexican tiling in front of it. To perk up the windowsill, I glued painted Mexican tiles to the top of the sill and adorned it with indoor plants: African violets, coleus, and wandering Jew (a prophetic choice?), all of which thrived in the good light. On the wall facing my bed, Lisa had painted a mural of a fair maiden wearing a wreath of flowers, wandering through the forest with a bird on her shoulder.

I copied Lisa in many areas. She tied colorful ribbons to the buttons on her jacket, so I did too. She liked to embroider, spin yarn, and dress up for the Renaissance Faire, so I did too. In eighth grade, I even convinced myself that I had a crush on the same boy she had a crush on. Lisa would come over to my house after school, and we'd make thick milkshakes with Baskin-Robbins chocolate mint ice cream. After pouring them into tall silver soda glasses, we'd eat them with silver soda spoons while we talked about our mutual crush on Michael.

Being a vegetarian provided something I didn't know I was seeking. Placing restrictions on what I ate gave me a sense of control over my life. I often felt overwhelmed by all of my choices, and having limits, at least in this one area, provided a comforting container.

I had been plagued for years by suicidal thoughts. When I was seven, I remember thinking I was the unhappiest person in the world but that I couldn't know for sure if I was the *most* unhappy person since I couldn't really know what other people were feeling. At the time, I also wondered whether I would shoot myself if I had a gun. Although that memory has been imprinted in my mind, I know I wasn't miserable all the time.

As a teenager, when the words "I wish I was dead" would periodically pop into my head, I'd try to shoo them away. When the image of a knife cutting the tender part of my forearm snuck into my thoughts, I'd try to ignore it and focus on something else. I was still hopeful that someday things would change and I'd no longer be so depressed.

I promised myself that I wouldn't kill myself before I reached the age of twenty-one. I had a feeling that something good would happen by then. But if nothing changed and I was still depressed then, well, we'd see. I had friends at school, but no close friends I could talk to about how I was feeling. I often rode my bike into Westwood Village. Riding around past streams of people without talking to anyone, I felt invisible. When I'd return home, I'd sometimes vaguely wonder if I even existed.

Sometimes I would ride past the bookstore hoping to see Jonathan, but I never went in again. One afternoon while I was riding my bike on a nearby side street feeling particularly depressed and invisible, I closed my eyes and kind of hoped a car would hit me. I figured that although I wouldn't actively kill myself, if it happened to me, I could live with that.

I liked making things with my hands, which is something that my mother, who was a creative and skilled photographer, encouraged. When I was in eleventh grade, I found out about an arts and crafts school in New Jersey called Peters Valley School of Craft. They had a summer program where you could learn woodworking, ceramics, weaving, and more. I wanted to go. My mother was delighted I had found something that excited me, so she talked to the director, who told her that students had to be eighteen years old to attend. My mother replied, "Well, her birthday is in July." The thing was, I was turning seventeen, not eighteen, but I got to go. Sometimes my mother surprised me. At the time I thought of her as a total rule follower, but looking back, I see she was a quiet, behind-the-scenes rebel.

Nestled in the Delaware Water Gap National Recreation Area, Peters Valley was comprised of a collection of historic buildings set amid lush green hills, lots of wildflowers, and a little stream. My heart swelled with gratitude the moment I arrived. This was my kind of place.

Everything was different there. I was no longer invisible. I was part of a community. In high school I never had a boyfriend, had never been on a date. I doubted that boys even noticed me. But in Peters Valley, men took notice. I was tall and slender with straight hair to my waist. As a budding hippie, I often wore long, flower print skirts and Mexican embroidered blouses.

My woodworking course was in a weathered red barn at the far end of the town. Rather than taking the road there, I loved walking the back way—through a field and over a bridge that crossed a small stream. Every day I'd stop on the bridge and sing a song by the Incredible String Band to the stream and to the one yellow flower on the bank of the stream. The hollow, gurgling sound of the water flowing over the rocks soothed something deep inside of me. That walk, that stream, that flower, it all felt sacred.

Me (center with long hair) with friends at Peters Valley.

When I signed up for the woodworking course, I told the director that I planned to make a spinning wheel. It would be cool to have my own wheel. I knew how to spin yarn and had a spindle at home. Plus, I liked the idea of making something unique. Word soon got around that a sixteen-year-old girl (busted!) from California was going to make a spinning wheel. This was a big deal. They weren't used to having students from so far away, and making a spinning wheel is not a typical woodworking project.

When I walked into the woodworking barn on the first day, the teacher, Adam, looked up in surprise. "Are you in this class?"

When I nodded affirmatively, his eyes lit up. A few days later, standing in a field under a full moon, Adam and I kissed. He was the first man I had ever kissed. He was eleven years my senior and told me I seemed so wise for my age. While I may have possessed some wisdom, I think I came across that way because I didn't say much and people could project all kinds of things onto me.

I was also very innocent. Adam and I spent the night together the next night, but when he wanted to have intercourse, I was shocked and pulled away. He found a new, older, more experienced girlfriend a week later. I had been intoxicated by his attention and was hurt by his rejection. I pined for him for a long time, even though I didn't really like him very much.

The kitchen and dining area for the school took up the bottom floor of an old house. Nancy and Ricky, a married couple in their twenties, lived in the house and were the cooks for the community. There was a large vegetable garden in the front yard. We dined farm-to-table, long before it was trendy. Sometimes a few of us sat on the front porch and helped Nancy shuck corn or remove peas from the pod.

I liked to walk barefoot through the fields of wildflowers, and when I would return to the porch with splinters in my feet, my friend Kathy would gently dig into my foot with a needle to get the splinters out. I remember that time fondly, even the splinter removal. Kathy tenderly holding my foot, the sun on my face, the ancient tradition of women gathering together to shuck corn and tell stories.

At the end of my two-week woodworking course, I wasn't ready to leave Peters Valley. I felt embraced by a community. I loved the garden, hanging out on the front porch, the wildflowers, my little stream. I called my parents and asked if I could stay for the rest of the summer. They were grateful I was happy and said I could. But as the end of summer neared, I still wasn't ready to go home. I didn't want to return to LA, to high school, to my old life.

This time I had to convince my parents as well as my high school to give me school credit to stay at Peters Valley. My father always told his four daughters that he would pay for anything that was educational or that improved our relationship with one another. I persuaded my parents and the private progressive high school I attended in LA that this was educational.

Peters Valley was not designed to be a school during the non-summer months. Twelve artists lived there year-round, and they were working on their own projects. I would be the only younger, non-professional artist. I made arrangements to live with Ricky and Nancy. Ricky would act as my English teacher, giving me books to read and papers to write. I would use the science textbook my LA classmates had been assigned.

I went back to LA for a few weeks to get my stuff and buy winter clothes. When I returned to Peters Valley, it was virtually deserted. Of course the summer students were gone, but so were some of the resident artists, who had taken time off and not yet returned.

I sat on the front porch of the house where we had gathered for delicious meals all summer—the same front porch where Kathy removed splinters from my foot, where I felt I finally belonged. The house was empty now. I was alone, desolate. What had I done? Why did I push myself into doing things out of the ordinary, always trying to be special, different? Why couldn't I be satisfied with going to high school like everyone else my age?

I stayed in Peters Valley until February. It was a damp, cold, and extremely lonely time. I had planned on weaving that winter, but with no one else in the weaving studio, I dreaded spending time there, so I rarely went. I returned to LA for the last few months of my senior year of high school. I was depressed and wanted to see a psychotherapist but was embarrassed to ask my mother. None of my friends saw therapists. It wasn't common back then. When my mother finally suggested it, I readily agreed.

In my therapy sessions, I lay on the couch while Dr. R sat behind me. He hardly said a word. This was not helpful. How could I bond with someone who was invisible and never said anything? How could I feel seen if I couldn't see him?

When it was time for me to go to college, Dr. R didn't think I was ready, but I went anyway—to Fairhaven College, a small liberal arts school in Bellingham, Washington. Leaving home didn't feel like a big deal since I'd already left home once. And the first few months at Fairhaven were refreshing. "Dr. R was wrong," I thought. "This was all I needed. To get away and be with a like-minded community of people my own age. So much better than therapy."

Then I was seduced by Jason, the married resident supervisor for my dorm. Jason was also a professor at

Fairhaven, and he lived in the bottom-floor apartment right under my room with his wife and two kids. One evening Jason asked if I'd watch his kids while he and his wife took a sauna. When they came home, Jason said he'd walk me back to my room, which was one safe flight up the stairs.

Jason and I had been in an off-campus massage class together, and when we got to my room, he offered to give me a massage so he could practice the techniques we'd learned. I invited him in. My room was a single. With no roommate and plenty of privacy, I spread a towel on the floor and removed all my clothes, except my underwear.

As you might imagine, the massage turned into more than a massage. A year after my night with Adam in Peters Valley, I was no longer as innocent, although I still hadn't had sex. When Jason wanted to have intercourse, I didn't object. He was kind and gentle, but I didn't feel safe. Aside from the fact that he was thirty-five and married, I hardly knew him.

The next morning, I craved the comfort of close friends but had none. I was conflicted by what happened the night before and had no one but my journal to confide in. Jason and I continued having sex several times a week. He told his wife about us, and she was fine with it. She had someone else she was gaga over. But I still felt sleazy every time I walked past their apartment.

After a few months of sleeping with Jason, I didn't know how to extricate myself from the relationship. Around that same time, which was the end of the winter quarter, I got sick. One rainy afternoon I lay in bed with terrible stomach cramps, and I called my mom. After talking for a while and drinking in her motherly concern, I blurted out, "I want to come home." My words surprised me. I didn't even know that's what I wanted. I took a leave of absence from school and went home for a month to recuperate. That's how I ended things with Jason. When I returned to Fairhaven, I moved out of the dorm.

The whole time I was at Fairhaven, I took very few academic courses. Instead I took classes like beekeeping, organic gardening, and sailing. I even took a class on Chinese communism where we worked in the community garden together, while one person read to us from Mao's Little Red Book as if we were a Chinese collective. We clearly had no idea what was actually going on in those collectives.

I had some friends, but no close ones. My interactions with men were confusing and uncomfortable. There were no limits and no rules regarding if and when we should have sex. If I liked someone and they came on to me sexually, sometimes it scared me and I'd withdraw. Other times, I'd sleep with someone right away just to get past the tension of wondering whether we would or wouldn't have sex. I liked how sex sometimes made me feel powerful, knowing I had something that the guy wanted. I wasn't secure enough to believe he wanted me just because of who I was.

My classes started to seem like a waste of time. I didn't know what to do with my life, and the world of men and sex overwhelmed me. After two years at Fairhaven, I dropped out. More than anything, I yearned to discover my life's purpose. I tried this and that, but nothing stuck. The only thing I knew for sure was that I wanted to get out of my parents' house and out of LA. With all my belongings packed in my car, I headed north and ended up in Sebastopol, a rural community roughly two hours north of San Francisco.

I found a cozy chicken coop to move into. Fortunately, the chickens had moved out. It was technically a duplex chicken coop, with another living space attached to the far wall. In addition to me and my duplex neighbor, three other people lived on this eleven-acre piece of land. One lived in the pump house, and two were in the funky little main house with the shared kitchen and bathroom.

The chicken coop I lived in in Sebastopol.

My chicken coop had a wood-burning stove but no windows. When spring came, I found an old framed window, cut a hole in the wall, and set it in place. I worked at a fabric store that winter and spring, then I moved to Montana for the summer to work in the kitchen at a crafts school.

Though I had no plans for the coming fall, I was sure I would receive some kind of message about what to do next. I didn't know whether it might arrive through divine revelation or through the US mail. Every day that summer I ran to the mailbox, and every day I was disappointed.

When summer finally ended and my message hadn't come, I moved to Santa Rosa, which wasn't far from where I'd been living in Sebastopol. There was a junior college there, so reluctantly, I made plans to go back to school. That is how I ended up at Santa Rosa Junior College, for a few days at least, until I met Lucy outside a phone booth and she lured me into life as a Moonie.

Act Two

In the Moonies

(1975–1981)

4

Living in the Ideal World

After I accepted Lucy and Dina's invitation to stay and help The Family build a Heavenly Kingdom, that was it. I didn't board the school bus that departed from Boonville that night. Of those who did get on the bus, some were visitors, like I had been, and the rest were Family members who were returning to one of the Family-owned houses in San Francisco or Berkeley.

That left about fifty of us on the farm. Both Ann and Lucy stayed. Ann was assigned to "take care of" me even though Lucy, since she was the first one to meet me, was my "spiritual mother." Everyone had a "spiritual parent" and a "spiritual birthday." My spiritual birthday was September 15, 1975.

Lucy asked a Family member going to the city to stop by the place I had been staying and pick up my clothes. I left my car where it was because I had borrowed it from my cousin, and since he'd be returning soon from his trip to South America, he could pick it up. I'd figure out how to get the keys to him when the time came.

Jumping right into life on the farm was uncomplicated. There wasn't much I needed to deal with in the outside world. School wasn't an issue since I didn't care about returning. Saving the world was way more important. I'd call my parents later in the week to let them know my plans. I had no friends I needed to notify because I didn't even know anyone yet in Santa Rosa. There was nothing holding me back.

Monday morning at 6:00 a.m. Ann whispered in my ear, "Hey Ellen, wake up. Let's take a hike and watch the sunrise." I shook myself awake. Realizing where I was, my heart fluttered with excitement. "Okay, give me a minute."

We tiptoed out of the Green Trailer, then scrambled up the steep hill behind the exercise field. Panting, we mounted the top of the hill, where we met the sun creeping over the distant hills. The sun warmed the chilly September air. Ann took my hand as we stumbled through a Cat Stevens song, mumbling the words we couldn't precisely remember.

"Morning has broken, like the first morning …"

My glorious first day in the Family. I hugged Ann in gratitude.

Though the weekday schedule was more relaxed then the weekend one, it still didn't leave much private time. The singing sisters woke us at 7:30 a.m. We were encouraged to "jump it," an insider's term for jumping out of our sleeping bags and proclaiming, "Good morning, Heavenly Father." I was willing to do a lot of things, but that wasn't one of them.

Then came exercises, breakfast in small groups, a lecture, and lunch. In the afternoons we had a work period with each group performing a different task—gardening in the large vegetable garden, picking apples in the orchard, cleaning the bathrooms and dwellings, or cooking meals for the whole camp. I enjoyed the work, especially picking apples. We picked the low-hanging fruit by hand and had tools to reach the apples in the upper branches. Once in a while, I got to climb the trees. When I was little, we had a fig tree in our backyard. It had big knobs on the trunk that served as a great ladder into the branches. I loved climbing that tree.

We often sang while we worked, which meant we hardly had time for one-on-one conversations. Plus, there were rules about how to interact. Dina cheerfully explained, "We have found that people get the most out of their time here if they give one hundred percent, join in all of the group activities, and only talk about the things that inspire them. When someone talks with negativity, it spirals and brings everyone down. We're creating a new kind of community. The Boonville way is no negativity."

Most of the members and guests were between the ages of twenty and twenty-six, from middle- to upper-middle-class, well-educated families, and ninety-nine percent of them were white. Some, like me, had dropped out of college, and most had been too young when they joined the Family to have completed their higher education. I would guess that prior to joining the group most members would have described themselves as politically left-leaning, open-minded, dissatisfied with the status quo, and searching for a better way to live. They were probably naïve and definitely not streetwise. Catherine was a bit older than most. When she turned thirty, I remember thinking that she was over the hill.

In the late afternoon, everything slowed down for ninety minutes of silent meditation. The Family had no formal meditation practice, though we were told to spend at least thirty minutes in prayer. If we had never prayed before, we were told to just try. During this time, we could wander anywhere on the six hundred acres but could not talk to anyone else. Thank God, no older Family member would follow.

This was my favorite part of the day. Alone at last. The first few days I walked through the autumn-colored hills but still felt unsure about talking to God. During her lecture the first weekend, Catherine had assured us, "You don't have to believe in God to be here," but the weekday vocabulary gave a very different impression. God wasn't just in the lectures, He was mentioned everywhere—in prayers, songs, and daily discussions. I can't count the times someone had said to me or written me a note saying, "Heavenly Father loves you."

It was amazing how quickly I got accustomed to it. Even though I wasn't sure what God meant for me or how to talk to God, the word no longer made me bristle. I was willing to accept the possibility. It wasn't that prior to coming to the farm I was an atheist. I just didn't know, and it wasn't a big focus of my life. I was searching for meaning but not necessarily for God. I thought the only people who regularly talked openly about a personal relationship with God were Christians. More specifically, a particular type of Christian, the type who tried to push their faith on others. I didn't want anything to do with that kind of person or that kind of God. If I had known that's who I would become, I would have fled Boonville on the Sunday night bus.

I wanted to call my parents and tell them about this magical place. I wanted to let them know I had dropped out of school, let them know where I was, and share my excitement. I asked Lucy several times if I could call home, but she kept putting me off. There was only one pay phone on the farm, and it was on the front porch of the White Trailer. I couldn't very well make my call on the sly. Besides, I figured they must have a good reason for the rules they'd come up with.

I'm not sure why I was so quickly able to accept the rules without question, especially since I had been pretty stubborn most of my life. While growing up, if anyone in my family asked me to do something, I rebelled. It had to be my own idea. I used to love making special coffee drinks for my father, with chocolate chips in the bottom of the cup. But if he asked me to make him a cup of coffee, I scowled and did it grudgingly.

Although I was frustrated by the farm's phone policy, I didn't make a big deal out of it because I was in awe of the promise this group offered. If you follow these rules, you can be part of a loving community, live in a beautiful place, and save the world. I wanted that so badly that I repressed my resentment over rules that didn't make sense to me.

Still, I felt a duty to call my parents, so I'd continue to ask Lucy when I could use the phone. Finally, she relented, quickly adding, "But I need to be there with you. Sometimes parents just don't understand, and I want to be there to support you if you need anything."

"Oh, you don't have to worry. My parents will be happy I found what I've been looking for."

I put a dime in the phone and asked the operator to make a collect long-distance call. My mother answered.

"Hi El. Thanks for calling to wish us a good Yom Kippur."

"Uh, yeah." I'd totally forgotten it was the holiest day of the Jewish year.

"I can't talk long because we're getting ready to go to temple. Did you find a place to rent?"

"Well, that's why I'm calling. I found this wonderful community."

"Hold on, let me put Daddy on." I could hear her call to my dad, "Hal, pick up the other phone. It's Ellen."

"Well, if it isn't the woman from Glocca Morra. Hi pal." My dad always answered the phone like that or with some other strange phrase. I never knew what it meant.

"Hi Dad. I was just telling Mommy that I found this wonderful community. It's up in Mendocino County."

"Mendocino County? How are you going to get to school?"

"I'm not going to school. This community is just what I've been looking for. I'm going to stay here."

"What do you mean you're going to stay there? For how long?" My mother's voice was now trembling.

"For a while. Don't worry, Mom. These people are great. There's no drugs or sex or any of that stuff."

I could hear her crying now, and she didn't cry often. I didn't understand why she was so upset. At the time, I hadn't heard of cults. They had not yet proliferated. This was before the mass Jim Jones suicide. But there had been the Manson family and all their horrendous murders. And the SLA had kidnapped Patty Hearst the year before. Maybe my mother was thinking about that.

My dad took over. "Ellen, you just met these people. Take some time to think about it. Just promise us that you'll think about it for a week or two before you decide to stay."

"Okay, I'll stay two weeks, and then I'll decide." I only said that to relieve their anxiety. I already knew that after two weeks I'd feel the same way and I'd want to stay forever.

My mother had stopped crying, though her voice was still shaky. "Ellen, I don't want to have this conversation when we're in a rush. Where can we call you when we get back from temple?"

I turned to Lucy. "What's the phone number here, so they can call me later?"

She looked apologetic. "Sorry, no one can call in on this phone, and we don't have another."

Now I was feeling torn. "Um, Mom, this is a pay phone and you can't call in on it. They don't have any other phones here. But don't worry, I'll call you next week. You'd really like it here. And Dad, you'd love it. We sing a lot of songs. Don't worry, I'll be fine."

"Okay, we have to go. Make sure you call soon," my dad said.

I felt guilty for leaving them hanging like that. And I felt guilty that my mom's first assumption was that I had considerately called to wish them well on Yom Kippur, when I hadn't even remembered it was Yom Kippur....

Norman and Sally were in charge of the weekday training sessions at Boonville. I came to understand that the training sessions, designed to recruit people into The Family, were the primary purpose for having the land. However, the property also had a large vegetable garden and an orchard that provided produce for The Family's consumption. Another Family member managed those.

Norman, a slender Jewish man with dark hair that was thinning on top, delivered the lectures. Someone told me he used to live on an island and had hair down to his waist. That was hard to picture. Now he dressed like an accountant, bland and boring, in dark-gray slacks and a white long-sleeved, button-up shirt, with a white short-sleeved undershirt peeking through at the collar.

Sally was in charge of logistics. She appeared gentle and easygoing when she played her guitar and led the group songs, but behind the scenes, she shouldered a huge responsibility. Not much older than I was, she managed everything to enable the training sessions to run smoothly. And they ran very smoothly. Every minute was planned, with one activity on the heels of the previous one. Each staff person knew how to orchestrate their group, and every member quickly learned their place in the hierarchy as well as how to manage the potential new recruits in their charge.

One afternoon several days into my first full week at Boonville, Sally took me aside. She was dressed in her typical "uniform" of a knee-length skirt, cotton blouse buttoned almost to the top button, and her hair pulled back in a ponytail. Her tennis shoes were dirty because the area around the trailers was always either dusty or muddy. We sat on a log, dangling our feet, talking in the sun. She told me how glad she was that I was there and that she was sure God had a special mission for me. I felt handpicked, like a little kid with a crush on her teacher, and her "love bombing" cemented my resolve to stick around.

Love bombing was a powerful practice used to encourage people to join and remain loyal to The Family. Just as it sounds, Family members intentionally went out of their way to shower love on each new recruit or "spiritual sprout." It wasn't necessarily insincere, but the purpose was clear—get people to join and remain with The Family.

My first month in The Family, I was definitely seduced by the love bombing. But it didn't take long before I became one of them, and I did what was done to me. Soon I was recruiting new people and love bombing them.

As soon as the bell rang for meditation on the afternoon after Sally love bombed me, I took off into the hills, which were covered in long wild grasses dotted with small purple and yellow wildflowers. I found a hidden spot far from everyone else. Kneeling, I gazed toward the ground and hesitantly spoke to God, as I had attempted to do for the past few days.

"Heavenly Father, I don't know if you exist. But if you do, please let me know."

The shapes and colors around me came into sharp focus and the rigid walls of my heart gently loosened, like crystallized honey melting on a warm day. The small patch of grass in front of me transformed from generic "grass" into individual blades in subtle shades of green, gold, blue, pink, and brown. As I studied the tiny world in front of me, a fluorescent orange bug climbed up and down through the forest of grass.

The exquisite details shook me awake and I began to cry, overwhelmed by beauty and palpable love. *This must be God.*

It wasn't a particular ideology that attracted me to The Family; it was the love bombing, the beautiful surroundings, and living and working together toward an idealistic goal. While Norman gave a lecture in the Chicken Palace every day, the lectures mostly went over my head. I picked up things here and there, but I was too overwhelmed to digest the content. If I had heard the same lectures in a dingy environment with apathetic people, I may have backed out the door on day one.

Plus, if I had heard of Reverend Moon or the Unification Church prior to going to Boonville, if I'd known that Creative Community Project was a front for the church, that the bulk of my life in The Family would not take place on this beautiful farm but back in the city and that I'd become a closed-minded, religious zealot, I would not have accepted Lucy's invitation to dinner.

The lectures were the foundation of the community, supposedly written by divine inspiration. Attending them was required. Over the course of the week, Norman described how God created an ideal world, how it fell apart, and how the second coming of the Messiah was going to put it back together. Each week unfolded in an identical manner.

On Monday, we learned about God's ideal world. It was a fantastic, inspiring vision. Who wouldn't want an ideal world? We all could see we weren't there yet, and in the lectures that followed, Norman would tell us what went wrong and how we could fix things.

Tuesday was about The Fall of Man. In the beginning, Adam and Eve lived joyfully in the Garden of Eden. Since they were children, their love had not grown to maturity. Not until they were fully mature would they have a direct link to God's love, and not until then were they to procreate. That was essential because this direct connection to God is what would provide them with the capacity to love their children unconditionally and raise them properly to maturity.

Unfortunately, Satan seduced Eve before she was fully mature. Then Eve seduced Adam. Since Adam and Eve's children were born before their parents were directly connected to God, Adam and Eve couldn't properly love their children with God's love, so their children became part of Satan's lineage rather than God's. Ever since then, humans have been disconnected from God and unable to love unselfishly and unconditionally. Our world was in desperate need of someone who descended directly from God—a Messiah—to reconnect the rest of us to God's lineage.

On Wednesday, we heard a story about Jesus that was different from everything I'd previously heard. Growing up as a Jew, there were references to our waiting for the Messiah to bring the ideal world. According to Norman, Jesus might have had the potential to be the Messiah, but since his own people (the Jews) didn't accept him as the Messiah, he wasn't able to accomplish his mission. Thus, it was imperative that another Messiah emerge to finish the job.

On Thursday, Norman drew a timeline on the blackboard, marking off significant biblical events. This was the grand finale lecture. The timeline "proved" that another

Messiah would come, and he would be born in Korea in the year 1920. Left with that cliff-hanger, everyone stood up and sang a forceful rendition of "Marching on Heavenly soldiers, marching on with His love …"

The first time I heard this lecture series, so much went right past me. It didn't cross my mind that according to this timeline, the Messiah was alive right then. I don't know how I missed that since it was the whole point of the lecture.

Although I had attended religious school until I was fifteen, I didn't recall much about the Old Testament, and I knew far less about the New Testament. When Norman presented the timeline of biblical events, I took his word at face value. I was naïve, idealistic, and so desperate to find my purpose that his historical account seemed plausible.

5

Twice Chosen

My second week in Boonville the Thursday history lecture bowled me over. The Messiah was here on Earth at this moment! Did anyone know who he was? Was he connected to this group? No one said.

You may be perplexed at how I could accept the idea of a Messiah so easily. I've often wondered if being Jewish made me more susceptible. There were a lot of Jews in the organization, and since Jews comprise less than two percent of the US population, the high percentage of Jews in The Family was noteworthy. Growing up a Reform Jew, we didn't talk much about a Messiah and we didn't envision God sending one individual to save humanity. I recalled that we were awaiting the messianic age, and my (perhaps flawed) understanding of the concept was that human beings collectively would eventually figure out how to create a peaceful world. There was no denying the world was a mess, and I was very encouraged by the prospect that a living, breathing Messiah could help us put it back in order.

Throughout my first few weeks on the farm, I felt secrets lying behind closed doors, and I had a sense that there were some things I wasn't supposed to ask about. So I didn't. After all, living in Boonville felt like a slice of Heaven to me. I wasn't going to let a few secrets bring me down.

My group leader, Dina, was vivacious, enthusiastic, and cheerful—a blend of qualities that usually drove me nuts. I often judged people who were super energetic and cheerful as shallow. But Dina was different. I felt emotionally safe with her, as if her container was deep enough and strong enough to hold me.

Our group met after the lectures each day to discuss and share insights. We were encouraged to ask questions, but not all questions were treated equally. Family members, especially the staff, provided cues as to the appropriateness of a question. When someone was moved or inspired, we clapped for them. When someone was doubtful or critical, we did not.

Following each lecture the actions and attitudes of the longtime Family members set the tone. Were they jubilant or mournful? Should we clap or weep? Throughout each day, Family members intimated which behaviors were commendable and which were not. Mirroring them, we newer Family members would adjust our behavior to fit in.

While this doesn't differ much from how people strive to be accepted by families and social groups, it was remarkable how the Moonies were able to radically change our behavior in such a short period of time. Maybe it was because we were surrounded by our peers, all of whom essentially said, "Before I joined The Family, I was just like you. I was searching. I tried everything. This is the answer. I am happier than I've ever been. You will be too if you stay with us." This spectacular prize motivated me to follow the rules and mold my behavior.

We also were encouraged to make a concerted effort to examine our shortcomings so we could improve our character. To build an ideal world, we needed to become ideal people. Dina asked us to identify three things we wanted to change within ourselves and then set three goals to change those things.

It didn't take much digging for me to see that judging and comparing were my constant companions. Was I deeper or was I shallower, was I more interesting or was I boring? When I had compared myself to my peers in the past, I usually concluded that as an introvert, I was more introspective and thus deeper, but I also worried I was boring. I craved feeling special, unique, or unconventional. I didn't believe everyone could be special—there simply wasn't enough specialness to go around. By my logic, others had to be "less than" for me to be enough. I reluctantly acknowledged my arrogance.

We were encouraged to share so much in a group setting about our internal world—our connection to God, our search for meaning, the aspects of our character we'd like to change. As group members opened up, I initially wanted to prove that I felt more deeply than they did, but I soon recognized this was a defense mechanism provoked by my insecurity. I also realized that while in the past my judgments had kept me at a "safe" distance from others, they also kept me feeling profoundly lonely. With everyone around me being so vulnerable and open, I pledged to stop comparing myself to others and to overcome my arrogance.

Late one Friday afternoon I was invited to go on a hike with about twenty other people. The sun cast long shadows across the tall golden grass, and we were told to be silent as we climbed a steep hill behind the camp. On the hilltop, Sally laid out a few blankets for us to sit on, and Norman told us to get comfortable—he was going to tell us a story. We huddled together while he told us about a poor Korean man named Sun Myung Moon. Norman spoke with familiar intimacy, as if he was letting us in on a secret. I'd never heard the name before and had no expectations about the story.

Norman explained that when Sun Myung Moon was young, he was very religious. One day Jesus came to him in a vision and explained that he wasn't able to finish the job God gave him because the entire world had not accepted him as the Messiah. Jesus asked Moon if he would take over the mission and finish the task of saving the world. Moon refused. Jesus pleaded until Moon finally accepted the mission. Moon later channeled a doctrine and called it the Divine Principle. All the lectures in Boonville were based on the Divine Principle.

Dusk was setting in. After the story everyone was quiet. Most of the others already knew that Moon was the Messiah, but for me, this was the first time I understood not only that the Messiah was alive then but that we were his disciples. Incredible. I had been searching in vain for direction for so long, and at last I found it. What higher purpose could there be than to do the will of the Messiah?

Norman instructed us to go off and pray as a brisk wind charged the air. While I pensively walked away from the circle, I saw Sally take her coat off and give it to one of the shivering brothers. Without thinking, I took off my coat and gave it to her.

Something about the spontaneous generosity broke open my heart. I ran to an isolated spot among the trees, sat down on a log, buried my head in my hands, and let sweet, cleansing tears gush out. When I looked up, a brilliant full moon was glowing right in front of me. There is no way to explain what happened next other than to say I distinctly heard God whisper in my ear, "This moon is a present for you."

The most abundant, delicious, gracious love poured into me as I wept with gratitude and astonishment. This was unlike anything I had ever experienced. I was flooded with a love more profound than any human love. God felt intensely real.

I knew it was time to return to the group when I heard singing in the distance, but I wasn't ready to leave my embrace with God and the silver moon. I lingered a bit and by the time I reached them, everyone else was already standing in the circle holding hands. Two people released the hands they were holding and welcomed me in. I took their hands and became one with the others. As we sang "The Impossible Dream," I got completely choked up on the words. "To dream the impossible dream, to fight the unbeatable foe … To fight for the right, without question or pause. To be willing to march … for a Heavenly cause …"

The words pierced my heart, penetrating every shred of cynicism, fear, and doubt. I basked in the sweetest, purist, most noble love of goodness. Crying, I quietly promised God I'd remain at His side and do whatever He needed of me. I would strive with my last ounce of courage to dream the impossible dream and create the ideal world.

In the days that followed, I learned that Moon, the new Messiah, had accomplished something essential that Jesus hadn't. Moon had children. According to the Divine Principle, Jesus was supposed to have a family to help him save the world. This made sense.

Prior to joining The Family, even though I didn't believe that Jesus was the Messiah, I couldn't understand why a loving God would have his son die on a cross. That people worshipped the cross, the murder weapon of sorts, seemed even more bizarre. It made much more sense to me that Jesus, or now Moon, would have a family to heal the world.

My first month on the Boonville farm was the most glorious month of my life. I lived and breathed wonder, exhilaration, and peace, along with the unwavering clarity that my life's purpose was to work for the Messiah. In fact, I had been chosen for this sacred duty. (It was often emphasized that we'd been chosen). Really, I had been twice chosen. As a Jew, I was told I was one of God's chosen people. But this was different. At Boonville, we had a very specific mission. Being chosen by the Moonies was double proof that I was special.

On top of that, I finally understood why I had been tortured for so long by depression, beginning with my suicidal ruminations at the age of seven. God had been preparing me for my life as a Heavenly soldier. Reflecting on the promise I made to myself years ago that I wouldn't kill myself before I reached the age of twenty-one in case things got better, well, now I was twenty-one. I had made it. I no longer wanted to die. I was awed that God had been preparing me all along for this mission.

6

Not What I Signed Up For

The idyllic Boonville lifestyle didn't last. After a month on the farm, I was told it was time for me to move into one of the three Family-owned houses in San Francisco. At the end of that weekend's training session, I boarded the Sunday night bus with the others who were heading back to the city. Three hours later, past midnight, I was dropped off in front of my new home.

Walking up the steps of the house was disorienting. How could this be where we lived? It was a big, beautiful Victorian in the ritzy Pacific Heights neighborhood. The house was a shockingly luxurious contrast to our Boonville accommodations. I soon discovered, though, that even a three-story house gets tight when twenty people live in it. Although it wasn't nearly as crowded as the Green Trailer in Boonville, when you were living in the country, tromping through the mud, feeling drenched with God's love, and getting love bombed by the older Family members, living in tight quarters added spice to the adventure.

Lucy had left the farm the week before, and she greeted me with a hug at the front door. I was nervous. Where would I sleep? What was expected of me? Just as the cues in Boonville had begun to remold my behavior on the farm, I quickly learned that there were now more rules to follow in the city. The Family preached unconditional love, but, in practice, there were endless conditions for acceptance. I was relieved Lucy was there to guide me through my first few days.

She took me upstairs and whispered, "This is where the sisters sleep. The brothers' rooms are on the top floor." She walked me down a long hallway to an open door and signaled, "You can sleep in here. I'll be a few rooms away."

In the dark I could make out six or seven women asleep on the floor in sleeping bags. It suddenly struck me that I'd probably be sleeping on the floor for the rest of my life, or at least until we finished building the Heavenly Kingdom.

"See you in the morning. Wake up time is 5:15 a.m. Good night. Heavenly Father loves you."

5:15 a.m.? Why? That's crazy early.

After a measly four-and-a-half hours of sleep, I heard faint singing and sleepy voices mumbling, "Good morning, Heavenly Father." Someone gently shook me. "Ellen, it's time to get up. Chanting starts in fifteen minutes."

Chanting? What was that?

Everyone spoke in hushed tones as they washed and dressed. The house was built for a normal family and had a normal-sized bathroom. But there was nothing normal about this family. Ten girls politely jostled each other, washing their faces and spitting toothpaste into the sink.

As I pulled on my dirty jeans, I panicked when I noticed the others were all wearing white dresses or long white skirts with white blouses.

"I don't have anything white. I don't even have a dress. What should I do?" I asked the woman next to me.

"Don't worry. Those jeans are fine. We'll get you a white dress later. We only wear white dresses for morning prayer."

At precisely 5:30 a.m., twenty brothers and sisters stood in a tight circle in the prayer room at the end of the hall. The room had no furniture except for a small low table that held a picture of a man and woman in a gold frame and a tall emerald-green vase of lavender roses. The room smelled like honey. I figured the people in the photo were Reverend Moon and his wife, or as I'd heard some people refer to them, True Father and True Mother or True Parents.

A phrase from the Ten Commandments floated through my mind. "Thou shalt have no other Gods before Me." I brushed the words aside.

Everyone stood silently and a bit droopy from lack of sleep until Daniel, the guy from the farm, motioned for us to begin. Then they all started punching the air, one fist then the other, like they were hitting a punching bag.

"Glory to Heaven, peace on Earth, bless our True Parents," they shouted. I acted as if there was nothing strange about it and joined in.

"Glory to Heaven, peace on Earth, bless our True Parents." We repeated the chant seven times, and then we went on to the next one.

"Glory to Heaven, peace on Earth, bring one righteous person to training session this weekend." We repeated this seven times before moving on to the next chant.

"Glory to Heaven, peace on Earth, bring one millionaire to training session this weekend."

Bring one millionaire? Now this was getting really weird. There we were, a bunch of ex-hippies, anti-establishment, anti-materialists, chanting for a millionaire to join our Family. What did this have to do with loving people unconditionally and building the Heavenly Kingdom?

We chanted every morning at 5:30 a.m., and I dreaded it—both waking up at an ungodly hour and the chanting. We also were encouraged to chant to ourselves all day long. We were told it would help us maintain our focus, and it would encourage the spirit world to support us and prevent Satan from invading our thoughts.

After chanting we cleaned the house in silence. That was a pleasure compared to aggressively punching the air and bellowing we wanted a millionaire.

Next came the morning service, during which we'd gather around the long wood dining room table while Daniel read us an inspirational message from the Bible, the Divine Principle, or perhaps a poem. We'd then gather in our assigned groups.

My group leader was Iris, who seemed nothing like an iris or a flower of any kind. Small, thin, and angular with fine straight hair pulled back in a clip, Iris wore her long-sleeved blouse buttoned tight around her collar and wrists. Definitely not Jewish.

Iris and Daniel were the "central figures" for our house. God worked through the central figures, so they were always right even if we subordinates didn't see it that way. In addition to following the central figures' directions, we treated them with extra care. The person serving food at our meals would serve the central figures first, perhaps even adorning their plates with flowers from the garden. The central figures were given the most comfortable chairs with extra pillows. It was an honor to serve the central figures.

I cringe now as I recall how I behaved both toward the central figures in the Moonies and toward the first central figure of my life, my father. At the breakfast table in my childhood home, my father used to say things like, "Babe (referring to my mother), can I have some toast?" (This meant, get me toast.) I hated that he bossed my mother around and was even angrier that she complied. When I'd complain, she'd say, "You have to pick your battles."

On the occasions in which our family would vote on a group activity, my father would declare, "I get six votes and you each get one." It was a sad joke because it was true. I despised my father's superior stance, and everything inside me wanted to prove him wrong.

In stark contrast to my rebellious tendencies within my birth family, I quickly fell into lockstep at the service of the central figures in the Moonie household. Why? To suggest I was under mind control would be an oversimplification. My desire to live a purposeful life and save the world surpassed everything else.

I often thought it must be taxing for Iris to be Daniel's partner in leading the household. Daniel was warm, funny, and charismatic, and everyone loved him. Life with Daniel felt expansive and joyful, whereas life with Iris felt serious and confined. She stuck to the rules and to her determination to help us shape our behavior so that we'd be impeccable before God. It was obvious we preferred being with Daniel.

My first morning I was looking forward to a big breakfast of pancakes, eggs, or even a bowl of hot cereal. Anything would be better than the granola we had every day on the farm. As our group sat on the living room floor, someone passed around cups of orange juice. I kept peering toward the kitchen nonchalantly but didn't see any more food coming.

I was the only new person in the group, and Iris welcomed me to the "Trinity," which is what they called these groups, our family within The Family. Then she explained, "In our Trinity, we have decided not to eat breakfast. We only drink juice in the mornings as a small way to remind ourselves of all of the people in the world who don't have anything to eat."

"Now that you're living in the city," she continued, "you get to be part of the real work of building the Heavenly Kingdom. Every day we go out witnessing."

There's one of those Christian words again, I thought to myself. I didn't like the sound of it. I had images of Seventh-day Adventists coming to my door, dressed in dowdy clothes and handing me a cartoon pamphlet about the rapture.

Iris continued, "We witness so we can bring people to our house for dinner. Just like how Lucy invited you, Ellen.

We'll leave the house at 9:00 a.m. and go downtown to witness. We'll return together at 5:30 p.m., hopefully with a guest or two. Don't worry, Ellen, you'll have a partner to show you what to do."

Everything was different here. Getting up at 5:15 a.m. Chanting. Liquid breakfast. And now witnessing. I already missed the farm and the love bombing. What had I gotten myself into? I flashed back to the magical moments I was cradled by God's love at Boonville and reminded myself that The Family was where God lived. This strengthened my resolve.

At promptly 9:00 a.m. on a typically cold, drizzly San Francisco morning, we bustled out the door and into the waiting vans. Ten Family members piled in and headed downtown. We got out at the intersection of Powell and Market, adjacent to the trolley car turnaround and the BART station. By our clothes, you couldn't necessarily tell us apart from the other people milling around San Francisco. But most of us were dressed more conservatively than we had prior to joining the Moonies. Since we didn't have the opportunity to retrieve our former wardrobes, we made do with what we had. In mirroring Iris, we started buttoning our shirts higher and wearing longer skirts.

We were cruising for tourists because they were the easiest people to entice for dinner. We targeted those with backpacks since they typically were delighted by our invitation to a free meal. When you were looking for tourists, the intersection of Powell and Market was a prime spot since it was the beginning and end of the trolley line. Sightseers were jumping on or off a trolley or milling around waiting for the next trolley to arrive. Plus, with the crowds going in and out of the adjacent BART station that was a busy hub for people traveling between San Francisco and the East Bay, there were even more people to witness to.

We set up our recruiting table near the trolley turnaround. Next to the table we had an easel showing pictures of our farm and a sign that said *Creative Community Project*. Two of us would hang around the table, engaging people who walked by, while the other Family members went off in pairs to try to bring someone home for dinner.

On the farm I'd heard that Reverend Moon was the leader of the Unification Church, but I wasn't exactly sure about our connection to it. Was Creative Community Project part of the church? Reverend Moon was not yet well known in the US in 1975—as I mentioned, the first time I heard of him was at Boonville—but as he began garnering more press attention in America, it often wasn't positive. I don't remember when I realized that Reverend Moon and the Unification Church had an unfavorable reputation and that followers of Reverend Moon were referred to, in a derogatory manner, as Moonies.

Was I a Moonie? We were instructed to tell those who inquired that Creative Community Project was not connected to Reverend Moon. We flatly denied being Moonies. We said we studied Reverend Moon's teachings in the same way we also studied those of Jesus and Buddha, but from what I'd seen so far, that was a lie. We were Moonies. We did not study Jesus and Buddha, only Reverend Moon, because he was the Messiah.

But we lied with good intentions. We lied to save spiritual lives. We were taught that at some point everyone must follow the Messiah. I don't remember what the "or else" was, but I assumed it was go to hell. Catherine instructed us to think of it this way: If a baby is about to touch a hot stove, you grab her and pull her away. You don't stop to explain why; you save her first and explain later, when she's old enough to understand.

It was the same thing with bringing new recruits, whom we called "Heavenly Children." They may have heard lies about Reverend Moon, which would make them turn away from learning The Truth—Reverend Moon was the Messiah, he received direct revelations from God, and he had codified them in the Divine Principle. It was imperative that we saved people first and explained later. Their spiritual lives were at stake!

By joining the church, our Heavenly Children would have the honor of being among the first group of people to follow the Messiah. Eventually, the followers would not just be a small ragtag group of young people. If we worked hard enough, everyone would follow Moon, except those who denied the Messiah and went to hell. So even though I hated lying, Catherine's logic helped me justify it.

Iris took me under her wing. We walked down Powell Street, and while stopped at a red light, she started talking to the man standing next to us. "Hi, are you from around here?" Just like that, she launched into a conversation. He scowled at her as if to say, "Why the hell are you talking to me?" But she was not deterred. "We're having an open house dinner tonight. If you want to come by, here's an invitation." She handed him a slip of paper, just like the one Lucy had given me not much more than one month before. After we crossed the street, I saw him drop it in the trash.

Iris kept going. One person after another. She'd start up a conversation, tell the person about our community, and then invite them for dinner at our house that night. Some people seemed interested, and we'd talk for a few minutes. Some were not, and we'd move on. It was exhausting.

Around noon we went back to the table, where Iris gave us each a peanut butter and jelly sandwich. I sat on the low wall near the table, savoring a few moments of relative silence. I was halfway through my sandwich when Iris called to me, "Ellen, go talk to that guy."

What? She had to be kidding. I clenched my teeth, put down my sandwich, and resentfully ran after the guy she'd pointed to. I was pretty sure I wouldn't like being in Iris's Trinity.

For the next four years, I spent nearly every day doing many of the same things. If I wasn't witnessing, I was either on the farm with a "spiritual child" or traveling around the country selling flowers. Witnessing went against everything in my nature. I was shy, introverted, afraid of rejection, and hated being deceptive. Every single day of witnessing pushed me beyond my limits. As it stretched and challenged me, I grew increasingly confident in approaching and conversing with strangers. It was never easy or enjoyable, but after a while, I was good at it. People trusted my casual, non-threatening, and sometimes even playful manner.

We would witness from 9:00 a.m. to 5:30 p.m., then rush home to meet our guests for dinner. If we had a guest, we were supposed to shadow them the entire night, and that stressed me out. If I didn't feel a connection to the person, it was difficult for me to figure out how to carry on a conversation for an entire evening. Even though it was my sacred duty to bring home Heavenly Children, I was secretly relieved when I didn't personally have a guest to tend to.

The vans would deposit us back at our Pacific Heights home just before 6:00 p.m. so we could greet our prospective Heavenly Children. Right before guests started to arrive, Nancy would set up a card table immediately inside the front door. She'd cover it with a golden-yellow tablecloth, place a small glass vase of orange roses in the corner, and set out a basket for donations. As each guest arrived, she'd greet them.

"Welcome, please come in and leave your shoes at the door. Who invited you tonight? Can you give a dollar donation for dinner?"

If they didn't have a dollar or if they protested, saying that the person who invited them said the meal was free, Nancy would assess their character. Did they look like someone we wanted, or did they look like a homeless, mentally unstable, lost soul whom we could not save? If they passed the test, she said it was no problem and let them sail through without paying. If they didn't, she apologized and gently (or firmly) escorted them out the door.

We'd begin each evening in the living room where Family members and guests sang a few songs before standing in line for a buffet dinner. With our plates piled high with casserole and salad made with vegetables from our Boonville garden, we'd gather in small clusters on the carpeted living room floor.

After dinner, Daniel would give a talk similar to the one I'd first heard in the park in Santa Rosa. The talk where the three blind men encounter an elephant and each one thinks the whole elephant is just like the small part he can feel. Each man possesses only a fraction of the truth, even though they falsely believe they have the whole truth. Daniel would go on to explain that, in our community, we're looking for the whole truth. He wouldn't reveal that we already had it.

We'd then attempt to persuade our guests to go up to the farm for the weekend. The evening program ended at about 10:00 p.m. After all the guests were gone, we'd meet with our Trinity to share inspirations from our day. Whenever we had a snippet of free time in the evening, I'd write a letter home. Then we'd reconvene at midnight to sing and pray.

Most people did not hold back. The room shook with wailing, crying, pleading. Praying like this was not part of my religious upbringing. I didn't know where the tradition came from. I guessed that for most of the members, if they prayed at all in their family of origin, it did not look anything like this. When my family went to synagogue, which wasn't often, we recited Hebrew prayers out of a book. It was all very subdued. I didn't even understand Hebrew. At home on Friday night at the beginning of the Sabbath, we said Hebrew prayers over the candles, wine, and challah. Beyond that, we didn't mention God or pray. While it is part of the Jewish tradition to actively engage, argue, or plead with God, it's not something I ever had done on my hands and knees in a group setting.

Since I'd joined The Family and felt deeply connected to God, I liked to pray, but not like this. I couldn't concentrate. How could you pour your heart out when someone else was beating her chest, clamoring for God's forgiveness? How could you have a private conversation when you couldn't help overhearing the private conversation of the person next to you? How could you feel God's tender caresses with such a racket all around you? Only after the midnight prayers were we allowed to go to sleep, although the staff typically stayed up for more meetings. Five-fifteen a.m. rolled around very quickly.

While witnessing near a BART station one Wednesday, I noticed a man with a backpack riding up the escalator. When he reached the top, he looked around as if he was trying to get his bearings. His back was to me. Full of anticipation, I tapped him on the shoulder. When he turned around, my heart sank. He was dirty with a scruffy beard, and he smelled. We may have professed love for all people, but we really only wanted bright, middle-class, white, young people to join The Family. This guy looked homeless, and I didn't want him.

Still, I told him about our community and reluctantly invited him to dinner. Iris saw us talking and must have seen something in him that I didn't. She came over and suggested I take him home right away for lunch. Lunch? We never did that before. Why did I have to drag this guy home with me?

Paul was thrilled to be invited to lunch. He said he recently arrived in California from the East Coast and apologized for his appearance, explaining he hadn't had a shower in days. He took a shower at our house, which was a significant improvement, then we had lunch. Although I attempted small talk, I couldn't seem to generate sincere interest in him.

As soon as he learned about Boonville, he said he'd love to go. I pleaded with Iris for someone else to take care of him while he was there. It wasn't just Paul. I was still going up to Boonville nearly every weekend, and as much as I loved being there, going back and forth all the time threw me out of whack. I liked to stay in one place for a while, and leaving at a moment's notice felt particularly destabilizing. Iris granted my request, and someone else took Paul to Boonville that night.

That weekend I went up to take over his care. When I arrived, I was amazed at how he'd transformed into a gentle, hardworking man in just a few days, and I was ashamed at how quickly I had discounted him. He was deeply grateful to me for having saved him, although I hardly deserved it. With tears in his eyes, he confided that he'd come to California to kill himself, and if he hadn't joined The Family, he probably would have committed suicide.

I stayed with Paul in Boonville for another week, happy to be on the land again. I truly loved it there—the hills, stream, and especially my memories of my first month there. As I watched Paul continue to blossom, I was convinced we were doing significant good in the world.

Years later after I had left the church, I'd hear people say "they" did it on purpose. As in, "they" sleep deprived "us" so they could more readily brainwash us. But who were the "they" and who were the "us"? Most of the church leaders were regular folks who'd been invited to dinner and consequently left their previous life, just like me. Most of them weren't living in luxury. Most didn't sleep much either. We all believed we were serving The Truth. We worked hard because these were desperate times. God needed us. We were chosen. The real question should have been, "Who exactly was benefiting from our collective hard work and lack of sleep?"

7

We Are Your Family Now

It was always a big deal when Dr. Dugan and Minnie came over. We rolled out the red carpet, made them special food, and everyone was on their absolute best behavior. Minnie, one of the first members of the Unification Church, had started our Bay Area chapter. We considered ourselves to be more West Coast casual than the rest of the church, evidenced in part by the fact that we called ourselves a family rather than a church.

Nonetheless, we adhered to the church's rules regarding proper behavior, especially regarding relations between men and women. Upon joining The Family, we were to remain celibate until marriage. Oh, and Reverend Moon would pick our ideal mate and marriage date, but more on that later.

Meanwhile, there was to be no intimate touching, no smooching, no couples. In the rest of the church, brothers and sisters couldn't touch at all. Our rules in The Family were only slightly more relaxed in that we could hold hands when in a group, but holding hands as a couple was strictly forbidden.

Dr. Dugan had been a university professor when he joined The Family. He caught Minnie's eye, and they got married. (I'm guessing their marriage either pre-dated Reverend Moon's matchmaking process or he had sanctioned their marriage.) They were an odd couple. She was a demanding, intimidating Korean woman, while he was a kind, mild-mannered Jewish man. These were the leaders of our chapter, the Oakland Family.

Whenever the Dugans entered our house, Catherine would order us around. "Get them some water. Take their coats. What's wrong with you? Don't you know how to greet Minnie and Dr. Dugan?"

On this particular evening, Minnie, dressed in a pink suit with fur around the collar, sat down on the couch next to Dr. Dugan. He wore a suit jacket, and his thinning hair was combed over the bald spot on the top of his head. Family members gathered at their feet. Looking at us scornfully, Minnie said, "I saw a brother and sister holding hands at Fisherman's Wharf. It was a disgrace. I hope I never see something like that again."

Why did Catherine adore Minnie? What did Dr. Dugan see in her? I never saw Minnie behave in a warm, loving, or compassionate manner. And why, I wondered, did she have fancy clothes, a luxurious car, and a large comfortable home, when we slept on the floor and had nothing? I had heard stories of how she struggled to start the Oakland Family all by herself when she first arrived from Korea. But what about now? What did she do to further our cause? Why was she treated with such reverence?

Although I knew these questions were off the table, more forbidden questions began bubbling up inside me—like when the sisters decided to give up dessert while Minnie was trying to get pregnant. A logical person might wonder what one thing had to do with the other. Best I could tell, this related to The Family's views about "indemnity."

A lawyer likely would define the term differently, but this is how Catherine first explained it. "Let's say a little boy throws a ball and it breaks someone's window. To make up for it, he has to do something to repair the damage, maybe pay for a new window or do errands for the homeowner. The point of repayment, whatever form it takes, is for the boy to show that he is sincerely sorry for what he did. This payment is called 'indemnity.' On a cosmic scale, we have been hurting God since the beginning of humanity through our cruelty to ourselves and others. We must continually take actions to demonstrate to God that we are sincerely sorry."

According to this rationale, we could pay our indemnity with things like fasting or working extra hard. In addition to paying off the collective sins of humanity, we could also pay indemnity or "set conditions" to demonstrate our loyalty to God and our support for others. Setting conditions was like making a contract with God, and in The Family, we were often encouraged to set conditions.

For example, when I was witnessing, I often set small conditions. Sometimes I'd say to myself, "I won't go to the bathroom until I talk to three more people," or, "I won't eat lunch until someone says they'll come to dinner." In addition to whatever personal conditions we chose, we often set

Family conditions. For a while we maintained a rotating fasting condition so that someone was fasting every day. Each person fasted one day a week to pay indemnity for the sins of others so that former sinners would now be able to respond to the call from God and join The Family.

Further, it was strongly suggested that each Family member begin a seven-day fast on their spiritual birthday. Always determined to do everything I could, for three years in a row, I did this seven-day fast. That meant no food, only water. Each time I was a wreck. I couldn't stay awake, and when I went witnessing, I often fell asleep while talking to someone. No wonder people thought we were brainwashed zombies. I sure looked the part during those fasts.

In any event, it was within this context of paying indemnity and setting conditions that I began giving up dessert on Minnie's behalf. I was in the kitchen helping several sisters scoop ice cream and cut cake to serve to everyone, which was the custom whenever Minnie or Dr. Dugan came over. For me, the cake and ice cream were the undeniable highlights of their visits.

As I sliced the cake, Catherine pulled me aside. "All the older sisters are setting a condition to not eat any dessert until Minnie has a baby. You should join us." Feeling intimidated and with a sinking heart, I agreed to give up dessert even though it was one of the few remaining pleasures in my life. Of course, Minnie could continue to freely consume as much dessert as she wanted whenever she wanted. But in solidarity with the other older sisters, I promised God that I wouldn't eat any dessert until Minnie had a baby.

Several months later, during a Family gathering in which ice cream was served, I mournfully passed it up. Then I noticed some other sisters eating it.

"Weren't we supposed to give up all desserts?" I asked a sister enjoying her ice cream.

"All of them except ice cream," she cheerfully replied.

Really? Except I had specifically promised God that I would forego all desserts. I couldn't go back on my word even though it was a promise I felt forced into. I didn't even care if Minnie had a baby. Regardless, to keep my word to God, I didn't eat any dessert for three years.

Minnie never had a baby, but another Family member made the ultimate sacrifice and gave her own baby to Minnie. At last I could eat dessert again!

Not long after I arrived in San Francisco, *TIME* ran a big story on cults, saying that cult members were brainwashed, cut off from their families, overworked, and underfed. Prior to that, there hadn't been much publicity about Reverend Moon or the Unification Church.

After my disastrous phone call with my parents on Yom Kippur, I had managed to calm their fears. Although they were concerned about my involvement with The Family, they figured it was one of my more unique adventures—one I'd learn something from and then surely outgrow. But the article in *TIME* totally freaked them out, so I invited my mother to meet me in Boonville for a weekend training session.

She was an amazing sport. Without complaint, she slept on the floor in the Green Trailer, ate granola from a cardboard bowl, listened to lectures, sang songs, and experienced how

I was living my life. She commented that I seemed happier than I'd been in a long time and that I wasn't malnourished. She said she felt I was safe, but she was puzzled. Given how much I cherished my privacy as a child, got irritated by every noise, and never liked being told what to do, she found it bizarre that I now was stringently following all the rules and living in such close quarters with fifty other women. Even so, seeing me in my element in Boonville soothed her fears for the time being.

Thanksgiving was coming soon. Every year for as long as I could remember, my entire family spent the holiday at our cabin in Lake Arrowhead. They expected I'd be there that year as well. Having seen other members miss their own family events, I nervously asked Iris if I could go. After my mother's successful Boonville visit, Iris viewed my parents as tolerant and supportive. With the desire to keep them on our side, she said I could visit at Thanksgiving as long as I took a chaperone with me.

The Family often restricted contact between members and their birth families out of concern that once you were away from the group, your family or friends would try to persuade you to leave, you'd lose your faith, or worst of all, your parents would forcefully prevent you from returning. A chaperone would help lessen the likelihood of any of those disastrous events.

Unfortunately, I didn't get to choose my chaperone. Kathy, a syrupy sweet woman was assigned to go with me, and I was supposed to pretend she was my friend. I was determined to make a good impression and wanted to show my family how much I had grown and become a wonderful example of unselfish service. Every time my mother needed something, I'd say, "Don't get up, I'll get it." I was so sweet my whole family wanted to vomit. (My mother told me that after I left the church.) Where was the feisty, stubborn girl they'd known so well? Apparently, Kathy wasn't the only irritating one at the Thanksgiving table.

During our Thanksgiving family gathering at Lake Arrowhead, my sisters, cousins, and I restaged a childhood tradition, lining up by age on a fallen tree for a family photo. From left to right: Davia (née Kim), Rob, Jan, Jim, me, Donny, Judy, John, and Laurel (née Laurie).

Although my family was nauseated by my behavior during the Thanksgiving visit, they were relieved I had come home and seemed both healthy and happy. During that first year in the Moonies, whenever I called my parents, they would both get on the phone at the same time, each on a different line. But they had different styles and intentions. My mother was warm and nonconfrontational so that I'd continue to call home. She would tell me about family gatherings or about eating breakfast on the deck with the wisteria in bloom. In contrast, my father tried to convince me with logic and facts that the path I was on was not a good choice. He'd cite articles, the Torah, and other philosophical or historical books. Because my parents' approaches were so disparate, my mother often ended up in tears, afraid that my father's style would drive me away. Eventually they decided that when I called, they would talk to me one at a time.

For the next three years, I visited them every six months or so. Whenever a terrible article was published about Reverend Moon or the Unification Church, they'd get scared, but after a visit, they'd be relieved.

8

Love Everyone,
Just Not Too Much

Premarital intimate relations between men and women were strictly forbidden. Since the Divine Principle taught that the Fall of Man began with the premature sexual relationship between Adam and Eve, sex before marriage was akin to reenacting the Fall of Man. It was considered the worst crime possible. To help curb temptation, men and women were not allowed to be alone together.

When the time was right, True Father (Reverend Moon) would choose our marriage partner and bless us so we could have sinless children. So far, the time for matchmaking had not been favorable, and very few couples had been blessed with marriage. This kept us in crowded houses of celibate twenty-something-year-olds who were pumped up with hormones and severely repressed.

Images of male genitals frequently floated through my mind. I tried to push them away or ignore them. I acknowledged my past sexual sins. I screamed at Satan, though usually only silent screams such as, "Stop forcing these images into my mind!" Nothing worked. As if all this weren't bad enough, I started falling in love with Daniel and having sexual fantasies about him. I didn't know what to do. I feared I was the only one with such a perverted mind.

As much as I admired Daniel and considered him to be closer to perfect than any of the other leaders, I also was intimidated by him. Underneath his glowing public persona, I had no idea who he was on a personal level because I never had a one-on-one conversation with him.

Even platonic love and friendship were tricky in The Family. We preached love but rarely had time to speak personally with one another. We knew next to nothing about each other's past lives, which were referred to as our fallen lives. Getting to really know one another was a pleasure that would have to wait until the Heavenly Kingdom had arrived.

One night I slipped into the prayer room, kneeled down in front of the picture of the True Parents, and cried tears of repentance about my feelings toward Daniel. I pleaded with God, "Please, show me what to do." The next morning, to my immense relief, Iris asked me if I would move to our house in Berkeley. Ah, this is how God answered my prayer.

I promptly loaded my few possessions into two cardboard boxes and moved to our house on Hearst Street, next to the Berkeley campus. The huge house had been a fraternity house before the Moonies bought it. Right inside the front door were racks of shoes, since everyone was to remove their shoes upon entering. The main floor was stately, with dark-brown molding around the windows and doors.

Considering that thirty to fifty people lived there at a time, the house was in excellent condition and remarkably clean. We had several large, carpeted meeting rooms on the main floor but no furniture, so we always sat on the ground. The second floor was for the sisters, and the third for the brothers.

Whenever one Family member passed another, they'd cheerfully ask, "How are you?" To which the other would energetically reply, "Great! How are you?" As the months wore on, I got tired of saying I was great all the time. Because I wasn't. What's the point of asking if the answer is always the same—and probably not true?

As I sat in our morning Trinity meeting in a sleepy, cranky mood, Iris intoned, "Ellen, you have to smile even if you don't feel like it."

I wanted to strangle her. Why did I have to smile? There weren't any guests around. Couldn't we be authentic, even with each other?

"If you smile, you'll feel better. Besides, Heavenly Father's heart is already broken. We have to be the ones to give Him hope."

Self-pity, self-indulgence, and selfishness were signs of evil. We couldn't even complain to God because He was already so distraught with the state of the world. It was our job to comfort Him.

Although I met some wonderful people in The Family, honest relationships were rare, and not only because we spent all our time working to build the ideal world. The real problem was fear. So many topics were taboo. We couldn't express our doubts or our fears, not even to God. We couldn't complain about lack of sleep or any other stressors. We were forbidden to have romantic or sexual relationships or even to talk about sex. Our past was part of the fallen world, and we had to leave that fully behind as well.

The one person I could be myself with was Ted, who had joined the church a few years before me. We felt safe enough with each other to commiserate about our doubts and complaints. With most Family members, there was an implicit hierarchy based on when you joined the church. You were either spiritually older or spiritually younger. When I was with someone who was spiritually younger, I couldn't express any doubts about the church because I would be a bad influence on them. When I was with someone spiritually older, I hid my doubts and complaints for fear of being judged. This created an emotionally unhealthy community for obvious reasons, but I trusted Ted.

I usually got paired with a spiritually younger member to go out witnessing, which I dreaded. Having a partner was clumsy, especially a younger member. It was awkward enough to nonchalantly walk up to a stranger and pretend you're a normal person who's striking up a conversation, but to have two people approach together looked totally fake.

On a warm spring day when all the younger members were paired up with others, Ted and I went off to witness together at the pier near Fisherman's Wharf. Some musicians were playing the waltz in an open square, and we decided to dance. Back in high school my friend Amy had taught me how to waltz on a beach. Now Ted, with his handsome dark eyes and wavy hair, swirled me around the square.

No one else was dancing, so passersby were delighted to see what appeared to be a young couple freely enjoying their love. If we hadn't been in The Family, that might have been true. But now we were supposed to love everyone in general but no one in particular. Even so, I had to do something wild once in a while or I'd go crazy.

9

Eat Fried Chicken and Meet the Messiah

In the summer of 1976 for America's bicentennial, Reverend Moon was planning a huge rally at the Washington Monument. There would be music, fireworks, and a chicken dinner at Moon's God Bless America Festival, and he wanted thousands of people to attend and hear his speech. We were instructed to go back East and sell tickets to the event.

I was part of a group of thirty people chosen from our Oakland Family to sell tickets. We each gathered a few items of clothing and put them in a small backpack, paper bag, or cardboard box, whatever we had. Hardly anyone owned a suitcase. We left California and traveled across the country in a school bus. Three days of driving with no witnessing, no flower selling, and lots of nap time was a delight. Larry, a tall, lanky, playful guy, led our team. Every so often we'd stop at a park, run around, play dodgeball, swing on the swings, or simply hang out under the trees and enjoy not being cramped on the school bus. It was a rare and delicious taste of freedom and levity.

By the time we arrived on the East Coast, the ticket-selling campaign had only just begun. We joined forces with fifty other Moonies, who had been bused in from other states, for a total of eighty people on our ticket-selling team. Baltimore was our territory. Additional teams had been assembled in other cities close to Washington, DC.

Our team of thirty from Oakland stayed in a small house in Baltimore for the next few weeks. The first night we gathered in the living room for an orientation given by Larry and another group leader. Fortunately, the other group was staying somewhere else. We were in uncomfortably close quarters as it was with just us.

Multiple sheets of butcher paper had been taped together and pinned to a wall to make a tall graph of our progress. There was a black line drawn with a marker going from the bottom to the top of the paper. We had three weeks for eighty people to sell ten thousand tickets at three dollars apiece. There was a big zero written in red at the bottom of the graph and then ten thousand written in green at the top. There were tick marks along the graph for every hundred tickets sold. So far, only one hundred and fifty tickets had been sold. Our task seemed impossible.

We were divided into smaller teams. I was on Michael's team with four others from the Oakland Family. Michael drove the van and assigned each of us our own neighborhood. He would drop us off in the morning and pick us up later in the day. It was up to each one of us to figure out how to maximize ticket sales. We could go door-to-door or to other churches or throw a party—whatever it took to bring people to the God Bless America Festival.

I was bewildered when I was dropped off with a sack lunch for my first full day of canvasing. I had no idea where or how to begin in the predominantly white, working-class neighborhood of Hamden. It was hot and humid as I dragged myself from house to house, but no one was interested. A few people suggested that I come back later, but I doubted it was worth it. I didn't sell one ticket.

Then I was assigned to a black neighborhood, where I met a little girl who took me to all her friends' houses and got the parents to buy tickets. I quickly became known around the neighborhood, especially by the kids. They'd wave at me and say, "Hello, Miss Ellen," or, "My mother's home now. Wanna come over with the tickets?"

One evening I went to a small apartment complex and began knocking on each door. "Hi, I'm selling tickets to a big event at the Washington Monument. There's going to be music and firecrackers, and we'll provide a chicken dinner. It's only three dollars, or two tickets for five. Do you think you could come?" We weren't supposed to mention Reverend Moon. We were selling tickets to a party. No one would pay to hear a speech.

Halfway through the complex, I met a slender black woman wearing a robe and curlers. "Whatcha doing out there? Come on in and have a seat." I went into her apartment and told her about the great event.

"Honey, it's dangerous around here. I don't want you walkin' around here at night. Why don't you talk to the people during the day, and if you need to collect any money at night, tell 'em to give it me. Then you just come here and pick it up."

I appreciated the offer, but I didn't take her up on it. For the most part, I was only there during the day. Besides, I was pretty oblivious to my safety.

We had competitions throughout the campaign to see which team sold the most tickets. There were no rewards. It was just for the thrill of a competition. Our team was usually the top seller. My teammates and I gave each other nicknames. There was Idona Care, M.T. Zombeanie, J. Negovitch, and I had two nicknames—Spay Stout and Miss Stout.

We worked even harder and longer hours during those three weeks than we had back home. Since there were so many people in our small house, there usually wasn't enough time or space to shower. Sometimes we'd take a short break during the day and go to the YMCA, where Michael paid the fee for the use of the shower. One time I was so exhausted that I couldn't decide if I'd rather take a ten-minute nap on the bench in the locker room or take a shower. And the bench was just a flat piece of wood on legs. Hardly a place for a comfortable nap. But it called to me. On the other hand, this was the East Coast in summer, and I was sticky sweaty. I finally opted for a five-minute nap and a quick shower.

When our team won first place in that week's competition, the prize was a huge stuffed green frog, which I then took around my neighborhood and introduced as my good friend. The kids loved him. After that, if I didn't have the frog with me, the kids would ask, "Where's your green friend?"

One day I walked up to a house, stood on the front porch, and knocked on the screen door. No one answered. The door was open, and I could hear people inside. I knocked again but still no answer, so I walked in. Four large black men were sitting around the table playing cards. They looked at me like I was out of my mind.

One of the men said, "Sugar, what the hell are you doing? You're gonna get yourself killed. Around here you don't ever walk into someone's house like that. Promise you'll never do that again."

After promising I wouldn't, the man went on to say, "But I've seen you around, playing with the kids and that big green frog. You're amazing. You walk in like you know us. That's hard for anyone, but you're white! You know, you've got something really special behind you. It's people like you that change this world. Someday, I'm going to be like you." I floated out of there on a cloud of his praise. Look how far this timid girl had come!

The average number of tickets sold per day by members of the highest selling team was thirteen, and the most tickets any individual person sold in one day was forty-five. I was determined to beat the record. After ten straight hours of work the following day, I had sold thirty-nine tickets. Seven more to go. When I knocked on the next door, I was greeted with, "Sit down, have some dinner." But I urgently replied, "Oh no, I don't have time. I have to sell at least seven more tickets today." The couple insisted I sit down and relax, and since they only wanted to buy two tickets for themselves, they said they'd send their kids out to sell tickets while we ate dinner. While we enjoyed a delicious steak dinner, their children sold two more tickets for me. Energized by the nourishing meal and their kindness, I sold late into the night, netting fifty-seven ticket sales! As a group, we ended up sending 9,850 guests to the God Bless America Festival. I was amazed at the dual powers of goal-setting and hard work.

I won the individual competition for selling the most tickets overall, and the grand prize was a fishing trip with Reverend Moon. I had seen him a few times, but only in a large crowd from afar while he was on stage giving a lecture or leading a ceremony. And since his speeches were translated into English while he spoke in Korean, those didn't feel like a direct experience of him.

When it was announced that I would be going fishing with True Father, Michael called Minnie with the news. She instructed me to take two things on my trip—honeydew melon and Dramamine. True Father liked honeydew melon, and I would need the Dramamine to prevent seasickness while we fished for tuna on the rough seas. "Most important, do not speak to True Father."

I flew to Boston and was picked up and driven to True Parents' huge white colonial in the coastal town of Gloucester. (It was one of their many homes.) That evening I sat on the floor in their living room while True Father sat in an overstuffed chair next to me, True Mother sat in a chair across from me, and several others sat on the floor or couch around me. They all chatted, like normal people, about the movies, traffic, dinner, whatever.

I was so tired that I kept nodding off. I felt totally ashamed. Here I was in the presence of the Messiah—and I kept dozing off. But I couldn't help it. Finally, it was time for bed. We had to wake up at 5:00 a.m. to get on the boat.

The next morning, in the dark, we climbed down the rocky cliff in front of the house to True Father's boat. The crew consisted of True Father, three bodyguards, a woman who won the ticket-selling competition for her region, and me. I took my Dramamine and we were off.

Once at sea True Father disappeared into his cabin for quite some time. I told myself that he was probably praying or doing other serious spiritual work. I didn't want to consider that he might be sleeping. On deck I helped catch small fish that we'd use as bait for the tuna.

Time rolled on, and there wasn't much to do. I talked with the other woman and with the one American bodyguard (the others were Korean and didn't speak much English). I wanted to be a star disciple, so I decided to clean the kitchen. I cleaned and scrubbed and made the place shine. Good thing I'd taken the Dramamine because the noxious aromas of the cleaning solvents and the rocking of the boat made for an unpleasant combination. Then I went up to the top deck and fell asleep.

A little while later, I heard True Father, so I came down. In a deep, gruff voice with a heavy Korean accent he turned to me and asked, "Are you sick?"

"No," I answered.

"Strong sister, not sick."

I later heard that ninety percent of the people who go fishing with him get sick. I silently praised Minnie for the Dramamine.

That was the full extent of my one and only conversation with True Father. As he uttered those few words to me, I tried to summon the appropriate feelings. The Son of God, the essence of love, was standing right next to me. Why couldn't I feel anything? His love must be beyond me.

There was a big swivel chair in the back of the boat, and when True Father decided it was time to fish, he sat in the chair and the bodyguards strapped him in. He had a huge fishing pole, and he let the line drag off the back of the boat. He got one bite but didn't catch any tuna that day.

I had brought my camera and wanted to take a picture of True Father, but I wasn't sure if that was acceptable. While he was standing against the side of the boat, I crouched down on the other side and pointed the camera toward him when he wasn't looking. But he saw and motioned to me while saying something in Korean to one of his bodyguards.

Was I in trouble? I went over to True Father, and the bodyguard told me to stand on one side of him and the other contest winner to stand on his other side. Then the bodyguard took our picture. I still have the photograph.

My experience with True Father was disturbing. He uttered only a few words to me, and I didn't feel the magic I had hoped for. The most difficult part would be going home to my eager brothers and sisters who would want to hear glorious stories about how his presence changed my life. I could neither lie nor tell the truth, at least not the whole truth.

When I returned to Oakland, I focused my reports on the events of the trip to avoid revealing my disappointment and absence of emotion while in the presence of the Messiah. While I carried my disillusionment deep inside for the rest of my time in the church, I did an excellent job of suppressing it. I rarely let it rise to the surface, and I certainly never expressed it to another member of The Family.

My prized photo with Reverend Moon and another member of the church on the boat.

10

Aching for God

The best place to pray in downtown San Francisco was the bathroom of the elegant, historic Saint Francis Hotel on Union Square. There were marble countertops and soft white towels, but the toilet stalls were the pièce de résistance. With doors that went from floor to ceiling and curved handles with push-button locks, they felt like my own tiny, sound-proof prayer rooms.

Secure inside a stall, I might break down in tears about God's desperation to reach His children. I knew He loved all of us intensely, and I could feel His agony at the pain His children felt and the pain we inflicted on each other. I would cry and promise to work even harder to bring His children back to Him. I was convinced that if everyone could feel His love like I could, the world would be healed.

Other times, I would punch the air and silently scream, "Get out Satan! Leave me alone! Stop accusing me of nega-tive thoughts!" Although Satan was not part of my Jewish vocabulary growing up, I now saw his hand in anything that got in the way of Reverend Moon's holy work.

Often though, I was so fatigued that my bathroom stall prayers dribbled into nonsensical words as my head drooped and I fell asleep. Even though we were all perpetually exhausted, we didn't think the reason we fell asleep was because we only slept four hours a night. No, we had been taught that little spirit men were sitting on our eyelids, a trick Satan was particularly fond of.

Despite my devotion to The Family, I had a gnawing feeling that something inside of me, spiritually or psychologically, was not right. I felt a deep urge to call out to God, but the prayer room at home was too confining. Longing to feel my feet in the dirt, I snuck out of our house in the middle of the night, ran to a field across the street, and begged God, "Take me! Please take me completely, swallow me up, I'm yours."

My desire to merge with God permeated my entire body. It was yanking and pulling me closer and closer, but not close enough. I couldn't lose myself completely. I was still there, alone in the field, a separate being with my own free will. I wanted to be a slave of love, but I wasn't able to become one with God.

When the nagging feeling that something was wrong with me persisted, I made an appointment with Sherry, an older sister I trusted, to confide in her and receive spiritual counseling. We met in a restaurant, sat in a booth, and ordered coffee. I looked down as I tried to explain the feeling, and when I looked up, Sherry's eyes were closed.

"Sherry," I tapped her on the arm, and she shook herself awake.

"What, what, I'm listening, go on."

I continued talking until I saw her eyes rolling in a struggle to stay awake. I couldn't share my heart with someone who kept falling asleep.

As much as I wanted to be mad at her, I couldn't blame her. I had fallen asleep talking to people plenty of times. And others of even greater stature had done the same. Daniel, one of the "central figures" and the object of my infatuation, moved to our Berkeley house on Hearst Street several months after I did. By then, the worst of my infatuation had passed. Late one night several members sat on the bright-green carpet in his office for a meeting. He smiled an impish smile and said, "Excuse me, I just need to have a little conversation with the floor for a few minutes." Then he put his head down and closed his eyes. The rest of us continued meeting while he took a five-minute nap.

* * *

After living in Berkeley for a couple of years, I was transferred to our new house on Bush Street in San Francisco, where Catherine, one of the founders of the community, continued to maintain a position of leadership. This four-story house was the most elegant yet. I recall coming home one night for dinner without a guest and Catherine calling everyone who didn't have a guest into the other room. I wondered what kind of activity she had planned for us. We stood in a circle while she prayed an intensely moving prayer.

"Now go back out and find someone. If I were you, I wouldn't even stop for dinner."

I couldn't understand how the same person could move me to tears of awe one minute and be such a tyrant the next. It was during one of my periods of feeling particularly reverential toward Catherine that I asked her if I could give her a foot massage. She said that would be wonderful and that we could meet in her room after her staff meeting, which was after midnight prayer. I entered her room cautiously, sat on the floor, and leaned up against her bed. Around 1:00 a.m. she came in, utterly depleted. She lay down on the bed and I rubbed her feet. I was in Heaven. It was such an honor to be able to serve her, knowing how hard she worked for the rest of us. She fell asleep and I tiptoed out.

No matter what acts of service I performed, I continued to feel "off." It got to the point that when I tried to pray, I either felt nothing or I fell asleep. I longed to experience the connection to God I felt during my first several months as a Moonie. Maybe all my time on city streets was getting in the way of my deeper faith. As soon as I got a chance to get back out on our land, I took it. I hiked to the edge of the property, as far as possible from everyone there. Angry and agitated, I climbed a tree, purposely scraping my body against the rough bark. The abrasion felt good. Then I jumped down and snuggled into a dry ravine.

"God, I want to love. I need to feel you," I cried out. My heart was aching and yearning to touch, to connect, to merge. "I don't know what to do. I'm willing to do anything, anything. Just tell me what to do."

I have to prove my love, I thought. God must be first. I need to sacrifice something to prove to God that He is first. Abraham was willing to kill his son, Isaac, to prove he loved God more than anything. Who did I love more than anything? My family. I loved my family so much. Could I give them up for God?

Sobbing and wrestling with this, I decided I'd give up my family. I would never call or see them again. I crawled out of the ravine, wiped the dirt off my hands and clothes, and went to see Norman. When I knocked on his cabin door, he invited me in, and over tea and cookies, I told him my plan.

"I don't think it's such a good idea," he said. "There's no need to completely cut off your family, especially when they're positive, like your family is. It will only turn them against us."

I was surprised, let down, and also relieved. I thought I had found the answer. Fortunately, Norman was sensible, so I didn't have to follow through with my plan. This was particularly convenient because I had a trip planned to visit my family at our cabin in Lake Arrowhead.

I loved being there with them, and I also hated it. Sometimes I wished they'd cut me off and say they never wanted to see me again. Not because I didn't love them. That was the problem. I loved them, respected them, and felt so torn during our visits. I couldn't explain my dedication to the church to them. I couldn't explain what we were doing. I knew I was hurting them, and there was no way to resolve the conflict. Unless, and this occurred to me while I was in Arrowhead, I just imposed a break. Which I did. While we were together,

I said that I thought it would best if I didn't come home again for at least a year or two. In response, my father sent me this letter.

Dear Ellen,

Over the years, all sorts of derogatory statements have been made about the Moon Movement. You know that my feeling has been to disregard those statements because your objectives seemed laudable, your friends seemed to be nice people, Dr. Dugan had reasonable answers to my questions, and you seemed to be happy and to be learning and growing. You even said you were learning more than you would be learning in college.

Since this is the time in your life where it is not unusual to want to experiment and to have many experiences, Mommy and I have supported you. We were convinced that you were growing, and we hoped that you were learning.

Of course, we have been concerned for a variety of reasons. One related to your retaining freedom to think for yourself. I have repeated over and over again that no matter what happened, you should retain your freedom of thought and action, and no matter what the circumstances, maintain your will to doubt.

My admonition to you from the first time we talked about this on Washington Street was never to give up that wonderful, stubborn Ellen quality, that quality which would always keep you from blindly and unquestioningly following one leader.

I have been satisfied that your aims are to do good, love thy fellow man, work for justice, and generally follow the Ten

Commandments and the ethical principles of Judaism as expressed in the Old Testament and the Jewish and humanistic traditions you found in your own home.

An accusation I have often heard is that the movement tries to separate children from their families. I have always disputed this because it has been our experience that our relationship has probably been better than before you had joined the movement.

With what I have just written as background, maybe you can understand why I became so emotionally upset when at Lake Arrowhead you said, "Maybe it would be a good idea if I didn't come home for a year or two."

I must tell you it was a terrible shock to me that I still haven't gotten over. Let me explain to you why. The easiest way to lose your freedom of thought and action is to become isolated and insulated. Unless you spend a reasonable length of time completely away from the people and activities of your religious order, you are isolated and insulated. It is important to come home to maintain an intellectual and emotional link with the world outside of your community and to engage in dialogue with people you know love you, people who want to help you keep an open mind.

When you suggested that you not come home for a year or two, the suggestion was shattering to me because it seemed to confirm what others had said. "The movement tries to separate members from their families to substitute Father Moon for their natural father."

Then, Ellen, you provided some justification for the separation, saying that God told Abraham to leave his father's *house because his father was an idol worshiper. I looked up the passages in Genesis and discovered that Abraham at the time was married and was seventy-five years old. I hope you don't feel that by coming home, "the evil surroundings would contaminate you," as some commentators try to interpret God's admonition to the seventy-five-year-old Abraham to leave his father's house.*

Another concern is that your community is so much built around Moon and Minnie—Moon the Messiah and Minnie his disciple. Maybe my fears are groundless, but history within my lifetime has made me apprehensive of organizations of faith built around the "cult of personality."

Would my wonderfully independent Ellen give up her freedom of thought and action and subject her will to that charismatic leader?

Now comes the tragedy of the Peoples Temple and their leader Jim Jones. I find that those who wanted to believe in Jones, like his lawyer, Charles Garry, as well as psychiatrists who have studied the cults, like Dr. West at UCLA, strongly confirm the danger to well-intentioned cult members who give up their freedom of thought to unquestioningly follow the commands of their leader.

Ellen, I know you rarely read a newspaper. Therefore, I have culled from the extensive newspaper stories on this tremendous tragedy a few articles that you will find enlightening, and that you may want to discuss with your colleagues. People you meet on the streets will be talking about this tragedy, confusing your group with Peoples Temple, and you should be aware of what is being said. I think reading the articles and discussing them will be a valuable educational experience for you and the members of your community. Remember, "Eternal vigilance is the price of liberty."

Ellen, I promised not to bug you about coming home, and I also promise not to bug you if you do come home. I hope from what I've said in this letter that you can understand why I have been so upset at the prospect of your not coming home for a year or two.

Love,
Dad

11

Buy Flowers and Save Your Soul

Despite my father's compassionate, well-considered, and very wise letter—I see that now!—I continued to keep my distance. Being with my family challenged me and my beliefs more than I could handle.

After my trip to Lake Arrowhead for Thanksgiving of 1978, I was frequently on the road selling flowers for *New Educational Development*, another one of our names. I hated it. I hated lying about where the money went. I hated being rejected. Compared to flower selling, witnessing was fun.

We were told that the purpose of selling flowers went beyond simply making money. On a grander level, we were helping to restore all the money that had been used in Satan's world to God's world. When people gave us their money, we were helping them pay indemnity for their past sins.

However, if we ever spent the money that we made on ourselves, all the sins of the ancestors of the person who gave us the money would fall on us. Heavy. I was afraid to even take one dime to make a phone call. The money we made had to first go to our central figure and get blessed with holy salt. Then our central figure would give us a small amount to spend for food during the day. The remainder would go to Reverend Moon and the church.

After doing daylong flower-selling excursions around San Francisco, I was chosen to go on special missions, which were extended trips beyond California. Montana, Washington, Oregon, Illinois, New York, Michigan, and Texas were among the states I traveled to and through by van with my fellow Moonies.

Although the team leader for each trip would set the tone for that particular mission, we'd always work incredibly hard. We typically slept in the van, and each morning we'd pull into a gas station to wash up in the bathroom. Then we'd take turns reciting to each other an inspirational reading from the Bible or the Divine Principle or a poetry book. For breakfast (at least we got to eat breakfast on flower-selling trips), we'd eat cereal or yogurt in the van en route to our first stop of the day.

We'd get dropped off one by one all around town to sell the beautiful roses we had shipped in from Colombia and kept on ice in the back of the van. The roses came in red, pink, yellow, white, and once in a while, we had my favorite, lavender. When I was told it was my turn to exit the van, I'd wrap a huge bundle of roses in newspaper, and the team leader would give me directions—go down here, then over there, and I'll meet you at the corner of such and such at 3:00 p.m. so you can restock for the afternoon.

As my team took off in the van for their selling destinations, they'd yell out the window, "*Mansei!* Sell out!

Heavenly Father loves you." We knew *mansei* was a Korean word, but I'm not sure any of us knew what it actually meant when we shouted it like a victory cry. I later learned that it refers to the Mansei Movement of 1919, in which two million Korean youth rose in protest against Japanese colonial domination of their homeland.

Immediately after getting dropped off with my bundle of flowers, I would find an inconspicuous spot to pray. Then I had to face the day. Some places were easier to sell in than others. Office buildings were the worst.

I recall a day when I felt particularly vulnerable and leery of rejection. I stood at the entrance to yet another nondescript office park and told myself, "Just go in one office, then you can go outside and cry."

When I entered the office building asking if they wanted flowers and was briskly escorted out the door, I held myself together long enough to get outside. Then I went behind the building and wept. For myself, for God, for the people who didn't know The Truth. But mostly, to comfort myself.

Then I pulled myself together with a gently encouraging, "Just go in two more offices, then you can cry."

I continued like this for most of the day. When my team leader, Johnny, picked me up at 3:00 p.m., I had made about fifteen dollars, although I should have been making at least ten dollars an hour. I got in the van, put my money in the money bag, and recorded it in the book. Oddly, I didn't feel defeated because as tough as the day had been, I hadn't given up.

Johnny offered me a short break, and I sat in the front seat while we drove around picking up team members and dropping them off in new locations. It was a delicious luxury to sit in the van and do nothing except stare out the window for an hour. At 4:00 p.m. Johnny dropped me off at a new location. Cradling my flower bundle, I found a dingy alley and began to pray. Crouched upon cool cement steps, my heart crumbled. The difficulty of the day made a pathway for God to slide right in and fill me with compassion for myself and everyone around me.

Through deep prayer, I felt myself moving through the darkness, and I knew the rest of the day was going to change course. As soon as I went back out to sell my flowers, people started buying. It was effortless. People just appeared and bought. That afternoon I made two hundred dollars and met my goal for the day.

A similar scenario happened numerous times. Whenever I had a day that was absolutely awful, it would break open my heart to pray. And after making hardly any money during the daytime hours, I'd rake it in that evening. Weekdays we usually stayed out until 10:00 p.m. or 11:00 p.m., and on weekends until 2:00 a.m. Then we'd find somewhere to park the van, or we'd drive all night to the next town. The moment I crawled into my sleeping bag, I'd be overwhelmingly grateful that the day was over, and I could finally rest. I imagined God cradling me in His arms, rocking me to sleep.

Despite the challenges of flower selling, I appreciated that it brought me to people I'd never otherwise come in contact with. I particularly liked selling in bars with down-and-out patrons because they often touched my heart. One night in Seattle I entered a dingy tavern that had only five customers—a bedraggled man engaged in a lively conversation with himself, two drunk old guys who were trying to shoot pool without falling down, and an elderly couple at the end of the bar who appeared to be homeless. I approached them.

"Would you like some roses for your lady?" I asked.

"Naw, can't afford nothin'," he mumbled.

I could tell he had the heart to give, but he just didn't have the money. I hesitated because I wanted him to have the chance to serve the Messiah, and we were supposed to charge at least a dollar for each rose.

"Do you have a dime?" I asked.

"Sure, I gotta dime, but I ain't dumb. Roses is more than that."

I couldn't resist. "Well, we're having a special sale today. One rose for a dime."

The old man pulled himself up off the stool and motioned for me to follow him over to the corner. He rummaged through his dusty pockets and brought out one nickel and six pennies. As he handed me all of his change, he said, "I want to surprise my wife."

I carefully wrapped a rose in green tissue paper so the deep-red bloom peered out of the top.

The old man carried it back over to the bar.

Standing tall in front of his wife, he held out the wrapped rose and said, "Nellie, I got a little somethin' for you."

Nellie's face shed a million years and her eyes brimmed with tears as she unlocked her tired love. She kissed him and then glanced up at me and said, "He ain't brought me a rose since our wedding day. Thank you, honey."

In another town, I knocked on the door of a ramshackle house.

"Come in," I heard someone faintly call from inside.

I entered the house and almost gagged. A disheveled young woman lay on the couch, oblivious to her surroundings, while her baby crawled around on the floor scattered with trash, rotting food, and dirty diapers. This heartwrenching scene strengthened my determination to work harder for the Kingdom of Heaven on Earth.

Then there were the times I was moved by beauty. In a different small town, I stood on someone's front porch and knocked on the door. When no one answered, I rested a moment in the sunlight. Morning glories adorned the trellis above me. Heart-shaped leaves dangled down around me. Suddenly my heart swelled as I saw the leaves as Valentine's Day cards from God.

I was thrilled that one of our flower trips took us through Boulder, Colorado. I loved the mountains, I loved the town, I loved the people. When I was seventeen, my family had taken a backpacking trip in the Rocky Mountains, and ever since then I'd wanted to live near the Rockies. Now, as I stood on University Hill in Boulder, I proclaimed, "Someday, I will live in this town!" (And someday I did.)

In addition to flowers, we occasionally sold jewelry or candy. Candy was the worst. Everyone would say, "I'm on a diet," even though many of them needed to be and probably weren't. We also sold little cartoon character pins. We had Mickey, Minnie, Popeye, and several others. We pinned them on a thin board covered with black velvet so the colorful array of characters would "pop" in contrast to the black background. The board had a black satin piece of fabric attached to the top so we could flip it over to cover the pins when we carried them around.

One day I was dropped off to sell in downtown Buffalo, surrounded by office buildings that stretched in every direction. I entered the first building and went straight to the bathroom—not to use the toilet, not to pray, but to clean. I cleaned the sink with paper towels and wiped spilled soap and water from the counter. Cleaning office bathrooms was something I did often, rationalizing that if I gave first, something would surely come back to me.

After cleaning the bathroom, I got in the elevator and picked a random floor. I knew they'd kick me out—they always did—so I'd just have to evade the security guards as long as I could. I got out on the seventh floor and paused for a deep breath. My heart was thundering, and I felt as small and vulnerable as a snail.

Just before entering the first office, I prayed to be invisible so I could get past the receptionist. My only chance of making money was if I could get to the bigwigs in the offices with windows.

"I'm sorry, you can't go back there. I don't think you're supposed to be in this building anyway. Did you ask the security guards?"

"Yeah, they said it was okay."

I lied. I hated having to hide from and lie about the security guards, but I figured the bigger the challenge, the more it might mean that Satan was hiding a fortune from me. I wasn't giving up yet. I returned to the elevator and with sweaty fingers pressed the button for the eleventh floor. The doors opened and I walked down the hall. The receptionist wasn't at her desk, so I slid right by. As I walked down the inner corridor, to calm my nerves, I imagined that all the scary men behind their big mahogany desks were actually little babies in diapers. But I peeked in each office, and no one was to be found.

After scouting all the offices to my right and finding no one, I went the other way and heard voices at the end of the hall. The conference room door was closed, but I could hear several men talking inside. Clutching my black velvet board with cartoon characters fastened to it in neat rows, I knocked on the door.

A man called out from behind the door, sounding surprised at the interruption. "Who is it?"

I steadied myself. "There are some movie stars out here who want to meet you."

"What?" He didn't know what to make of my reply.

"There are some movie stars out here who want to meet you," I repeated, with a little more confidence.

He opened the door a crack. "What did you say?"

I pulled out my black velvet board. "See, here's Minnie and Mickey Mouse and their friends. The whole gang told me they'd like to meet you."

The guy opened the door the rest of the way and gawked in disbelief.

Signaling me to come in, he turned to his colleague and said, "George, can you believe this? Anyone who's got the guts to break into a meeting with a line like that gets my support. Let's buy some of these things."

It was a good day.

12

Undercover

Flower selling kept me busy and before I knew it, two years had passed since I had last seen my parents. True to my word, I hadn't visited them since Thanksgiving 1978 at Lake Arrowhead. Now, late in the summer of 1980, my parents asked if they could come visit. I felt ready, so I asked Daniel, the team leader, for his permission for them to come.

Once Daniel gave his approval, I asked my folks if they would take my whole team out for dinner. They said they'd love to. I was actually really looking forward to it. We never got to go out for nice dinners, and I was sure everyone would like my parents.

At the time, my flower-selling team was staying near Tarrytown, New York. Reverend Moon lived in Tarrytown and gave Sunday morning talks at Belvedere, the church's nearby estate. As a rare treat, we were going to attend Reverend Moon's Sunday service, then meet my parents for dinner that evening. What a wonderful day it would be.

Very early on Sunday morning, Daniel called me into a private room, looking very solemn. "We just received a call that your parents are trying to kidnap you."

"What? How do you know? Are you sure? I can't believe it! What should I do?"

"Let's go to morning service, and we'll see if there's more information by the time we come back. The main thing is, don't get in touch with them, and of course you can't meet them for dinner."

When we returned from the service that afternoon, I was told that a deprogrammer had been arrested, and police found evidence in his files that my parents had hired him to kidnap me that weekend.

Daniel and I started making plans. I would leave my fundraising team and move to another state. But first I'd just stay in a safe place for a while so my parents couldn't find me. That evening was dark and stormy. As angry as I was at my parents, I still wanted to call and tell them I was okay. But I was not allowed to use the phone.

My parents didn't know why I didn't show up with my team for dinner, and they waited for me all night. They later told me that they called the church's Buffalo center every hour to find out where I was. The highway was slick, and they were afraid I'd been in a car accident. After I left the church, I found notes my father had written throughout the night while they were waiting for me. "We called the highway patrol at 8:00 p.m. We began calling local hospitals at 9:00 p.m. We called the Buffalo center again at 10:00 p.m." I cried when I read his notes, imagining the pain I had caused them.

When my parents called the Buffalo center, the people there kept putting them off, telling them that they didn't know where we were. Around midnight, the church finally told my parents I was safe but that I wouldn't see them. My parents were now desperate to see me. It was negotiated that I could meet them under controlled conditions. We had to meet at the church-owned New Yorker Hotel, and I had to have a chaperone. Maria would come with me.

Maria and I sat with my parents at a booth in the coffee shop in The New Yorker Hotel. My parents were grateful just to be with me. They'd been afraid they'd never see me again. I was angry, defensive, and also a little thrilled by it all.

My mother explained, "At first we were planning to kidnap you, but that all changed. We hired this guy, but last week we got a call that he'd been arrested, so the kidnapping was off. I was so relieved. You know how I hate confrontation. Then we thought that since we already had plans to be with you, we'd just go to New York and have a relaxing time together. We were really looking forward to seeing you and meeting your team. We promise we will never try to kidnap you again."

My father pulled out an apple, a plastic, bear-shaped container of honey, and a knife. It was close to Rosh Hashanah, the Jewish New Year, and it's a tradition to eat apples and honey for a sweet new year. He cut us each a slice, and I ate mine though I wasn't really in the mood. Bodyguards escorted me out to make sure no one grabbed me.

I was glad the church wanted to keep me safe. It made me feel special, and it was confirmation that my service was truly valued. I spent the next week at the plush home of one of Reverend Moon's supporters. It was the first week in five years where nothing was required of me. I was thrilled to sleep a lot, walk along the creek, and lie in the grass on the expansive property.

When I was reassigned to the church's fundraising center in Houston, Texas, I decided to change my name as an extra precaution so my parents couldn't find me. Oddly enough, I changed it to Rachel Jacobson. I say "oddly" because although I wasn't consciously aware of it at the time, this name combined the Hebrew names of my paternal grandparents, Rose (Rachel) and Jack (Jacob).

I was very uncomfortable with my false name. I'd introduce myself as Rachel, and then kind of off to the side I'd mumble, "but that's not really my name." Even though I didn't want my parents to have me kidnapped, I also didn't want to cut off all contact with them. I continued to call them occasionally, but I no longer called them collect as I'd done ever since I joined the Moonies. And now when I wrote to them, to disguise the post office mark on the stamp, I sent my letters to our Buffalo center, and they mailed them from there for me. That did fool my parents. They thought I was still living in New York and not attempting to hide it.

Texas was like night and day from New York. Although our Houston center also had a Japanese leader, he was a much warmer person than the one in Buffalo, and he and his wife and child lived with us at the center. The team captains for our two fundraising teams both had originally joined The Family in the Bay Area. One, Paul, was my spiritual son from

Berkeley—the homeless man I recruited from the BART station. The one who credited me with saving his life. The other team captain, Sam, had a playful, boyish personality. I was on Sam's team.

I quickly discovered that Texans were so much more pleasant than New Yorkers. The first time I went into an office building in Houston to sell flowers, my body instinctively cringed with dreadful anticipation of New York receptionists and secretaries. But the secretary at the first office I entered exclaimed, "What lovely roses! Let me buzz everyone in the office and see if they want to buy any." When I didn't make any sales, she apologized. I just about fainted.

I also noticed other delightful things about Texans. They rarely asked whom I was selling the flowers for. If they did, I'd just say, "my church," and that usually satisfied them. Even if I said, "Unification Church," they usually didn't know what it was. On top of all that, this was 1981 and oil and money were flowing in Texas.

Even with all these benefits, we still worked really hard. We spent part of our time in Houston, but even more time on the road, moving from town to town. When we were in Houston, we slept at the center; when we were on the road, we'd get one hotel room for all the sisters and another for all the brothers. This was a significant improvement over sleeping in the van.

13

Matchmaker, Matchmaker, Make Me a Match

In the winter of 1981, official word came from the central office in New York: It was time for everyone over the age of twenty-one who had been in the church for at least three years to get engaged. We were to travel to New York where Reverend Moon would choose our marriage partner.

I was twenty-six and had been celibate for over five years by then. For the most part, I had trained myself to stop thinking about men and sex. I didn't know how I felt about the prospect of marriage, especially to a stranger. But duty called, and this was a huge duty and an even greater honor.

The upcoming matching ceremony in which Reverend Moon would choose our spouse was the first step toward The Blessing. The Blessing was about far more than marriage. It was the most sacred ceremony in the church, during which all our sins would be removed and we would be grafted onto God's lineage. Once we were blessed, our children would be born sinless. Our children would be the first generation of sinless children! The Blessing was the greatest gift Reverend Moon could offer. It is what would make it possible for us to fundamentally transform the world. However, if we left the church after being blessed, we would be committing the worst betrayal of the Messiah. The stakes were high.

The Houston center was abuzz as all the eligible candidates (about half of us) packed whatever warm clothes we had for our stay at the church-owned New Yorker Hotel. The last time I was there, approximately six months prior, was when my parents had tried to kidnap me. That now seemed like such a long time ago.

When I arrived for the three-day stay, I was told I'd be sharing a room with just one other sister. What a treat! The event also served as a mini reunion because many of my old friends from San Francisco and Berkeley were also there for the matching ceremony. Some still lived in the Bay Area, while others, like me, had been moved to other centers. Lucy, my spiritual mother, was there, as was Pam, my spiritual granddaughter. Pam lived full-time at the New Yorker Hotel (which served as housing for many of the New York City-based Moonies) because she worked at the hotel. She wasn't personally participating in the matching ceremony because she wasn't spiritually old enough.

The next day roughly one thousand people gathered in the ballroom at The New Yorker. The men were on one side, the women were on the other, and Reverend Moon stood in the aisle that separated us. He walked down the aisle, gazing first at the men and then at the women. We believed he could see our spiritual ancestors and that he was matching people according to God's cosmic plan. He would look over at the men, point to someone and say, "you," then point to a woman, "and you."

The couple would meet in the aisle and walk together to another room, where they would talk briefly and decide if they accepted the match. I thought, "What choice do we have? Reverend Moon is the Messiah, so his choice is God's choice. Who are we to question that?"

I sat in the crowded room for several hours before he finally pointed to me. The man he chose for me was a tall, handsome Mexican man. We walked nervously to the small room to talk.

His name was Jim and he lived in the Boston center. He was from a small town in Texas, where his father owned a bakery that was connected to their house. Our backgrounds couldn't have been more different.

"Well, what do you think?" I asked. "Should we accept?" I posed these questions only because Jim didn't broach the subject. My immediate impression was that Jim was a wimp, but if he was the one God chose for me, there must be some reason.

"I don't know, what do you think?" he replied.

"I think we should accept."

That was it. We were engaged.

I later learned that a number of people from the Bay Area refused their matches because Minnie had instructed them to only marry another member from the Bay Area. That shocked me. Was their allegiance to Minnie or the Messiah?

Jim and I left the room and went into the lobby, where couples were having their picture taken. Lucy was there with her handsome blond fiancé. I was amazed how much many of the people resembled their partners. After Jim and I had our picture taken together, I told him I needed to rest. We made plans to meet for dinner, and I escaped to my room, unable to admit out loud that I was miserable.

On my way to my room I ran into Pam. Even though she was my spiritual granddaughter, I didn't know her well because she had left the Bay Area about six weeks after she joined.

"Can I talk to you?" she asked.

I was tired and grumpy, but I said "sure" anyway. We went to my room and sat on opposite beds.

"I have to tell you something. I'm not sure how to say it. I know it's wrong, but I really like my roommate. We slept in the same bed last night, and I could feel Satan tempting me."

How could she bring this up now? I had just gotten engaged to a total stranger and my head was swirling. I wanted to curl up and hide, but I was afraid for Pam's spiritual life. Homosexuality was a sin.

"Oh no, you can't do it. If it's too hard to resist, you should get another room."

Just then my roommate came in, so Pam said she'd talk to me later.

As we had planned, I went out to dinner that night with Jim and Lucy and her fiancé. It should have been great fun since we never got to go out for a social dinner with friends. But the conversation was strained. None of us knew what to make of our sudden engagements, and what did we have to talk about besides fundraising or witnessing anyway?

We spent another awkward day together in New York. About an hour before I was scheduled to fly back to Texas, I sought out Pam because I was worried about her. I tried again to convince her that sleeping with a woman would destroy her spiritual life. She seemed to listen, but just as I was leaving, she said, "I think I'm going to do it."

Before I boarded my plane, I sent a picture of me and my fiancé to my parents. I wasn't looking forward to marrying this man. When I tried to imagine myself with lots of little kids, I was filled with dread.

14

Top of My Game

With no word on when the mass wedding would be, the nervous excitement from our New York trip and my anxiety about marrying a stranger faded away as life as usual quickly resumed in Houston. Since life as usual kept us perpetually busy, there wasn't much time to ponder a hypothetical future wedding. After all, we still had seemingly endless flowers to sell and countless people to save.

Not long after my return to Texas, I had one of the most unexpectedly delightful flower-selling days of my career. We had been driving through small towns in the southern part of the state when Sam told me that my town was coming up. He gave me ten dollars for my meals for the day and said he wouldn't be back to pick me up until late that night.

Sam pulled over to the side of the road at the entrance to the town of Woodland, Texas. The sign read: Population 6,727. "I'll pick you up in the center of town at nine o'clock tonight." As he took two buckets of flowers out of the back of the van, he suggested, "You might want to hide one of these for now and come back to get it when you sell out of the first one."

I tied my sweater around my waist, took the flower buckets, and waved goodbye. It was 8:50 a.m., and I smiled at the prisms the morning sun made on the dew. The air smelled fresh, like wet grass. Although the houses were sparse at this end of the road, I could see the town center not far away.

I was excited to have a whole town and entire day to myself. I felt like a powerful, independent warrior for God. This town was mine, and I would win it for God. I would save this town.

I hid one of the buckets of flowers behind a fence in the tall grass. Then I kneeled down and prayed. As I walked into town, I imagined a troop of benevolent soldiers marching behind me. I began singing, "Marching on Heavenly soldiers … marching on with His love …"

I walked toward town, expecting a quiet scene. But when I got there, I saw trucks, movie cameras, and huge lights. More than a hundred people were gathered around a trailer waiting for something.

"What's going on here?" I asked a man in the crowd.

"We're waitin' for Dolly Parton!"

People were looking a little droopy in the heat.

"How long have you been here?"

"A few hours. But she should be coming out soon. I'm not leaving until I see her."

Bizarre. Here I was in a little town in southern Texas, a movie crew was filming a Hollywood movie, and the locals were enthralled at a sight that had been commonplace to me growing up in LA. I went to school with movie stars. Heck, we lived down the street from the Beverly Hillbillies.

"What's the name of the movie?"

"The Best Little Whorehouse in Texas!"

The action was taking place in the town square. All the signs had been redone to look like they were from the late 1800s or early 1900s. The restaurant had frilly curtains and a soda fountain. Had that been refashioned for the movie, or was it always like that? Everything looked quaint to me.

It was fun to observe the cultural juxtaposition of the Hollywood people and the rural Texans, and since they didn't seem to know quite what to make of one another, I felt more comfortable with both. If the movie crew weren't there, I probably would have felt like the only outsider. But by now, I likely felt more at home in a small Texas town than they did. Plus, even though I regularly saw movie shoots all over town growing up in LA, I couldn't go behind the scenes to sell flowers to the cameramen like I could here.

After soaking up the moviemaking excitement for much of the morning, I wandered away from the center of town. As I got farther from town, the buildings were more run-down, there was litter on the unpaved streets, and dust circulated in the air. I sold flowers door-to-door until the late afternoon, when I went into a bar to rest and cool off a bit. I noticed a couple of men playing pool as I walked in and traded the bartender a rose for a glass of orange juice.

I noticed an old man in faded overalls at a table by the window. He had white, close-cropped hair and a couple days' growth of a beard. His skin was weathered and wrinkled, and his long bony hands had age spots.

"Mind if I join you?" I asked.

He smiled up at me with emerald-blue eyes as he said, "I'd be tickled pink."

"My cat died last night," he continued, with moist eyes. "I reckon you don't want to hear about my cat, but I sure will miss her. I got her the day my wife left me, gone off with a younger man. She was tired of an old geezer like me. Where do you think we go when we die?"

I was taken off guard. I knew exactly where we went. I knew the whole history of creation, God's intention for an ideal world, Satan's corruption of the world, and that now was the time of the second coming. But this old man's grief and vulnerability threw me off. I couldn't preach to him. He was so open, I couldn't barrage him with doctrine.

I just put my hand on his and held back my tears. Was I arrogant to believe that knowing The Truth gave me a monopoly on love? Although God had chosen me to serve Him, could this old man, with his eighty-something years of experience, have wisdom to share with me? Dare I learn from someone who had not yet accepted the Messiah?

I selected a lavender rose and placed it on his lapel even though I knew I shouldn't. It would be better for his soul if he gave something first, if he paid for the rose. But I prayed that God would forgive him. "Please don't judge him for his ignorance, and please accept his pure love as an offering."

When the old man and I parted ways, it occurred to me that even though he surely had never heard of Reverend

Moon, he seemed more genuinely caring than anyone I knew at the church. Yet as quickly as that unsettling thought arose, I batted it away and took off to sell more flowers. I continued working all afternoon and into the night. My last stop was a crowded bar on the edge of town, where Sam was going to pick me up. I still had plenty of roses from my second bucket to sell and about an hour until Sam was due to arrive.

I decided to take my time, schmooze with the folks, and hope the flowers sold themselves. Having experimented with various selling strategies, I learned that in certain environments, it was better not to push the flowers. I might push the first few to get things rolling, and then I would pretend as if I didn't care. It worked at this bar. The flowers went slowly at first, but then more and more people came up to me.

"Hey, give me a few of those pink ones."

I rolled the pink ones up in paper and watched the guy present them to a young woman. Since men tend to be competitive and like to outdo one another, I hoped some other guys had noticed. Fortunately, they had.

The next guy said, "I'll take half a dozen of the red ones." He promptly presented them to his girl.

Right after that, another man came up and said, "Well, give me a whole dozen for my sweetheart."

Five minutes before Sam pulled up, I was out of flowers, and my heart was full of love for the people I had spent this magical day and evening with. I went outside, raised my arms to the sky, and praised God, the stars, this town, and the ability to love.

When the van pulled up, I jumped in, empty-handed.

"I sold out!" I cried. Then I collapsed on the pillow behind me.

* * *

Back in Houston, one of my favorite places to sell flowers was at a bar called Baby Jane's. Located on Westheimer Road, Baby Jane's was known among the Moonies as a notoriously difficult place to get into. One Saturday night Sam dropped me off on Westheimer so I could work my way up to Baby Jane's, then down smaller streets of neighborhood bars.

By the time I got to Baby Jane's it was about 9:00 p.m., and I hadn't yet made much money. I was determined to get in, but I knew I had to do so carefully, so I stood in the field behind Baby Jane's and prayed. Then I removed one beautiful long-stemmed rose from my bundle and went around to the front.

The bar looked like an old-fashioned saloon, with a wide porch that wrapped around the front and one side. A large, nicely dressed woman was sitting on a porch swing by the front door. I figured there was a good possibility that she was Baby Jane. I climbed the few steps up to the porch, smiled at her, handed her the rose, and promptly walked in. I didn't want to take the chance of asking her if she was Baby Jane or if I could enter, in case she said no. With feigned confidence I walked in, yet was nervous all night, wondering if the woman or the bartender might kick me out. But no one did. I figured either that *was* Baby Jane or Baby Jane wasn't there that night.

I returned to Baby Jane's the following Saturday night. Before entering I removed another long-stemmed rose. Since no one was sitting on the front porch, I looked for the large woman as soon as I entered, and I spotted her sitting at the bar. I walked over, smiled, and handed her the rose. With a slight smile and a heavy southern accent, she said, "Thank ya."

After that I sold my flowers, and no one kicked me out. I was pretty sure I'd found the key. She must be Baby Jane.

I also was making steady progress at the other bars and restaurants on Westheimer. There was one restaurant, in particular, where clientele drove up in limousines, Mercedes, and BMWs, wearing everything from rhinestone evening gowns to blue jeans, or a cross between the two, rhinestone-studded blue jeans.

Since all the cars were parked by valet, I had a captive audience when people leaving the restaurant waited for their cars. I stood to the side of the front door under the overhang, holding my flowers where they were obvious to see. The most I ever said was, "Flowers?" This was definitely a venue where it was best not to be pushy.

In fact, it was a great, relaxing place to make money. There was no threat of getting kicked out since I was already outside. I didn't have to push my flowers, no one was rude to me, and, most importantly, they bought flowers. I had a couple of regular customers, one of whom was Ralph, who bought flowers for his wife every time they came. Ralph came out of the restaurant alone one night when I was selling red silk roses instead of the usual fresh ones. Ralph started chatting with me, asking me who I was, whom I was selling for, and what religion I'd been raised with. When I told him I was Jewish, he got very upset. He was Jewish too. What was an intelligent Jewish woman like me doing here selling flowers for the Unification Church?

I enjoyed talking with him, but meanwhile other customers were coming and going. I began to raise my pointer finger to him to pause our conversation every time a potential customer walked by. Ralph didn't like this.

"I'm talking to you," he said. He was a bit drunk, but not obnoxiously so.

"I know, but I have to keep selling my flowers."

"How much for all the flowers?" He waved his hand over the boxes I had stacked behind me.

"One hundred dollars."

Ralph took out his wallet and handed me a one-hundred-dollar bill. "Now, don't talk to anyone else while I'm talking to you."

He asked about my parents and how they felt about me being here. He seemed genuinely upset, and I felt for him. We talked for another five minutes, then he took his boxes of roses and went home.

The next time I saw Ralph and his wife at the restaurant, he wouldn't look at me. His wife told me that he'd come home the other night with all of his roses and told her my story. He was still so upset he couldn't talk to me. I was moved by his concern, and I missed the warm greetings we used to exchange. When I left the church, Ralph was the first person I wanted to write to and say I was okay. But I didn't even know his last name, much less his address.

Our team usually stayed in Houston a few weeks, then we would go on the road for a month or so before returning to town. Whenever we were in Houston on a Saturday night, I'd do my Westheimer run. Baby Jane had grown fond of me. As soon as I'd walk in the door, she'd call out in her thick Texas accent, "Thar's my flower girl." I'd hand her my best rose, then walk around the place and sell.

When I sold in bars, I was far less inhibited approaching people than I would be as my regular self. In a way I was acting. Also, I was doing it for God rather than myself. I'd go up to men sitting at the bar wearing cowboy hats, and I'd turn their hats around to get their attention. Once I even stood on a table and sang a song to the entire bar, which was particularly amusing since I can barely carry a tune.

As I went from table to table in Baby Jane's one night, I approached a rowdy group of college-aged kids. One smart-ass guy asked me in a sassy tone, "Are you a Moonie?" I ignored him because nothing good would come of answering.

"I'm gonna tell Baby Jane there's a Moonie selling flowers in here."

"Go ahead."

I wasn't sure if she knew I was a Moonie or not, and either way, I didn't know how she'd react. When the guy went over to Baby Jane sitting at the bar, I stood close enough to hear their exchange.

"Hey, there's a Moonie girl selling flowers in here. You gonna kick her out?"

"If you don't like my flower girl, you can just leave."

The guy slunk out.

* * *

Although we didn't receive a medal or prize for making a lot of money, we did get a little pin indicating our monthly average. The entire time I had been in Texas, my monthly average had been two hundred dollars a day, seven days a week. Weekdays I'd make much less, and I'd make up for it on Friday and Saturday. This weekly average earned me a green pin. To earn a white pin, I'd have to double my sales. It was a huge leap, but I was ready to try.

I was astounded by the power of my intention. Every day the next week, even when I had a crummy territory, I made more money than I used to. Saturday I was really cooking. I spent the day at the Houston Oilers football game selling cartoon pins and Oilers pins. I bought a ticket to get into the game, then walked up and down the aisles hawking my wares just like the hot dog vendors; the only difference was that they were there legally, and I was not. The trick was to stay in as long as possible. I knew I could make a hundred dollars an hour as long as I stayed in.

By late Saturday night I had $525. The most I'd ever made in one day was $595, and I was determined to break my record. At about 11:00 p.m. Sam dropped me off at the Hyatt Regency Hotel. Donning the twelve-dollar cowboy hat he had bought me at the drugstore a few days prior, I jumped out of the van with my flowers and pins and cautiously entered the lobby. I only had one chance here, and there weren't any other places around if I got kicked out.

The lobby was empty, so I followed the signs to the lounge, hoping it was bustling with people. I was disappointed to see just three people—one man sitting alone on the couch and two men at the bar. I went straight to the bar and asked for a glass of water. I was worried that if I approached anyone, I'd get kicked out right away. This way I could hang out for a bit drinking my water, and hopefully someone would approach me. I sipped my water slowly, but nothing happened. Finally, I got up and holding my flowers high, I started to walk toward the door.

"Honey, whatcha got there?" called the man on the couch.

I walked up to him. "Flowers, pins, all kinds of things."

"Come here, sit down next to me."

I sat down and rested my flowers on the seat beside me. This guy was my only chance, but how could I make seventy-five dollars just from him? After a bit of small talk, I directed the conversation to my "expensive" new cowboy hat. I told him I paid one hundred dollars for it, but if he wanted to buy it, I might consider giving him a good deal.

"How much?" he asked.

"Seventy-five dollars."

"If you give it to me for fifty, I'll take it."

I pondered for a moment, then nodded affirmatively. "Okay. It's a deal." I took off the hat and gave it to him. Then I pulled out my pins.

"You might want to consider putting some hat pins on it as well."

He fingered through the pins and asked how much they were.

I usually sold them one for three dollars and two for five dollars, but there was no way I'd make another twenty-five dollars at those prices. "Five dollars each," I told him.

He picked out five pins and gave me seventy-five dollars for the hat and the pins. My heart was racing.

"I'll give this to my niece," he said, "I think she'll like it."

I like to think we both enjoyed the transaction. He probably knew I was bullshitting him on the price of the hat, but his money was buying him a few more minutes of companionship. I said good night and left the lounge.

There wasn't anyone else around anywhere. I had miraculously made my goal, so I sat outside under the beautiful stars and waited for Sam.

15

Kidnapped and Deprogrammed

On November 7, 1981, I was in a Dunkin' Donuts parking lot in Houston, selling red silk roses in glass tube vases. I had arranged the roses on top of cardboard boxes that I found next to the dumpster, hoping that cars passing by would see my display and pull into the parking lot to buy flowers. It had been a pretty slow Sunday, but I didn't mind. I was relishing the chance to take it easy. Every so often, I'd pack up my flowers and go into the Dunkin' Donuts, where I'd trade a flower for a cup of coffee. I had worked this parking lot before, and the girls who worked there were happy to see me and receive a free rose.

I had just returned from a Dunkin' Donuts coffee run and was rearranging my flowers, trying to get the vases to stand up straight on the flimsy cardboard-box table, when a big white van pulled up. Two guys got out and came to look at my flowers.

"Pretty nice flowers. How much are they?"

"One for six dollars, or two for ten. That includes the vase."

They bobbed their heads and made approving sounds. Then the side door of the van opened, and two more guys got out. They gathered around to see the flowers as well. I was getting excited about the prospect of a big sale.

There was a distinct shift in the air. The two new men didn't seem as interested in the flowers. They glanced across at each other, and all four men closed in on me and grabbed me. My screams pierced the air, and from the corner of my eye, I saw a waitress in Dunkin' Donuts gasp in horror.

Who were these men? What did they want? Were they going to rape me? They threw me in the van, jumped in, closed the door, and took off.

One of them continued to grip my arm tightly as I crouched down and coiled against the wall of the van. It was then that my father came out from hiding in the corner. He leaned over and reached out to touch me. "Don't worry. We're doing this because we love you."

I pulled back, seething with anger and fear. Oh my God, I was being kidnapped! My father hired these thugs to kidnap me!

I wasn't sure which was worse—rape or deprogramming. My parents had betrayed me, shattering the promise they made after the aborted kidnapping attempt that they wouldn't try again. I had believed them. I was devastated.

I held myself tight with my back to my father, absorbing the shock of his betrayal. Aware I couldn't escape from the van, I watched intently out the window so I'd know how to get out of wherever they were taking me.

*My father, inside the van used to kidnap me, next to the flowers I had
been holding when the deprogrammers grabbed me.*

After a while, the guy holding my arms spoke. "I'm Axel.
We don't want to hurt you."

Great, with a name like Axel he might kill me if I made
a false move. I tried to inconspicuously see if he was carrying
a gun. The church had warned us that deprogrammers were
violent.

"And that's Jeff, and the driver's Hank," Axel said gently.
"I'll let go of your arms if you promise you won't try to
escape."

Staring straight ahead I nodded a slow, glaring nod, and
he let go of my arms. I refused to look at or speak to anyone
during the entire two-hour drive. It was dark by the time we
pulled up to a little farmhouse that was surrounded by miles
and miles of empty fields. Another van pulled up behind us,

159

and another bodyguard got out. Five bodyguards were assigned to me, and we were in the middle of nowhere.

The farm outside Houston where I spent the first ten days of my deprogramming.

They took me inside, and Axel led me through the kitchen and living room and into a small bedroom. I immediately noticed bars on the window. The room had a single bed, a dresser, and two folding chairs. Under different circumstances, this would have been a sweet old house.

"Why don't you get some rest. I'm sure you're tired. Here, your mom bought you this."

Axel put a nightgown on the bed.

The mention of my mother made my silent anger rise again. Knowing she was part of this infuriated me more.

"Sleep as late as you want. We'll see you in the morning."
Then Axel left the room and locked the door.

I was tired, extremely tired, but I had to make a plan.
There was no way I was going to get out of here with five
bodyguards plus bars on the windows. I thought of Jane, a
fellow Moonie who had been kidnapped and returned to the
church several weeks later. She had gashed her arm with a
soda can so that she'd be taken to the hospital, then she surreptitiously communicated to the hospital staff that she was
being held against her will. When she came back to the
church, she had bandages up her arm. I could do something
like that. Maybe I couldn't get out the window, but I could
ram my arm through it. What other option did I have? I
would not allow these kidnappers to destroy my faith. I would
not be forced back into the world I had already rejected. I
would sleep now and wake at 3:00 a.m. to do the deed.

I quickly fell asleep and woke at 3:00 a.m. on the dot. My
purse had been securely wrapped over my neck and across
my shoulder when the kidnappers grabbed me, and they
hadn't taken my purse from me. I rifled through it and
removed the small photo I carried around of Reverend
Moon in an embossed gold frame.

Placing the framed photo on the windowsill, I sat on the
end of my bed, staring at Reverend Moon and praying for
courage. I knew to my core that this was a matter of spiritual
life and death.

I had just one opportunity to escape. If Jane could do it,
so could I. Over and over I tried to get myself to smash the

window, but I was immobilized by fear. This went on for nearly an hour. By 4:00 a.m. I knew I better act soon.

"Okay, this is it. I'll sing "Song of the Heavenly Soldiers," and on the last line of the chorus, I'll do it. Here goes … "Marching on Heavenly Soldiers, marching on with His love. Uniting in life eternal with our God in Heaven and Earth!"

Smash! I hit the window full force. There was a tremendous bang as my knuckles hit the glass, but it didn't break. Smash! I tried again, and it still didn't break. Maybe the third time's a charm. I closed my eyes, made a fist, and struck again. Glass shattered, and I felt blood running down my hand. When I opened my eyes, the windowpane was still whole, but the glass picture frame lay broken.

The door burst open, and all five guys pulled me back from the window. "What's going on?" they yelled.

Knowing it was useless to put up a fight, I retreated, lying face down in my pillow, while they boarded up the window. Then they removed the glass lampshade and bulb before leaving me alone again.

That was the most desolate moment of my life. I felt completely abandoned by God. I had spent years being cursed, persecuted, and rejected by people for my witnessing and flower selling, but I'd usually been able to find a back alley where I could reach out to God so He could comfort me. But now I couldn't find God anywhere, and I was terrified. Everyone around me, including my own parents, were from the other side. I had no safety zone. I was completely alone.

I eventually fell back to sleep. I heard someone open my door in the late morning and look in, but I pretended I was still asleep. I heard them leave, and outside my door some-one said, "Let her sleep. It's good for her to sleep a lot. Rest will help her get her senses back."

I slept off and on, not because I was still tired, but to avoid facing anyone. Around noon someone came in again. I couldn't sleep anymore, so I grudgingly acknowledged his presence.

"Do you want to get up now?" Jeff stood at the foot of my bed. He was big, tall, and burly.

"Yeah, I guess so," I growled back.

"Your sister Judy's here, so she can take you to the bath-room."

"I can go to the bathroom by myself."

"No, I'm sorry, you can't. After last night's episode, someone has to watch you."

Judy timidly entered the room. "Hi El."

This was hard. I loved Judy, and we'd always been close and honest with each other. I wasn't sure how to interact with her now.

"Hi." I didn't blame her as much as my parents, but she was part of this whole deal too.

She took me into the small bathroom, making sure I didn't try to cut myself with anything there. I used the toilet and took a shower, then she escorted me back to my room. There were some sweatpants lying on the bed, another pre-sent from my mother. I tried them on, but they were too small. In spite of my frequent fasting and limited food allowance, I had gained more than twenty pounds in the last six years. I figured my weight gain was due to the cheap, poor-quality food I ate, chronic sleep deprivation, and related hormonal disruptions. In any event, I just stayed in my nightgown.

Judy brought breakfast into my room. She scooted the folding chair next to my bed and sat with me while I ate. We didn't speak.

Now what? In what ways were they going to torture me? But something didn't feel right. We had heard stories in the church about the greedy, satanic deprogrammers. Although the guys here were big and tough, none of them appeared to be carrying a gun. Worse yet, they were all so nice to me. This wasn't matching my picture of how things were supposed to be.

After breakfast Judy left with my dishes, and a new guy came in. "Hi, I'm Ray Johnson." Ray took a seat in the folding chair.

I recognized his name. I had heard stories about him and his father, who were both deprogrammers. In fact, his father had deprogrammed several of the leaders from the Oakland Family. Ray was smaller and less intimidating looking than I'd imagined. He was thin with brown shaggy hair.

"I'm going to be talking with you for the next few days. You can listen or you can fight me, but you can't go anywhere, so you might as well hear what I have to say."

I didn't respond.

Ray started telling me things about Reverend Moon and the Unification Church. I'd heard it all before. This guy wasn't going to break my faith.

"Why does Reverend Moon live in a mansion and drive a Rolls Royce while the rest of you sleep on the floor and work ungodly hours?"

He wouldn't understand, so I didn't bother answering out loud. But in my mind, I defended the True Parents and my devotion to this way of life. Truthfully though, even though I tucked it far away from my everyday thoughts, Reverend Moon's privileged lifestyle had always been a sore spot for me.

"Did you know Reverend Moon owns a munitions factory in Korea?"

I'd heard that one too. I didn't know if it were true or not, but I didn't really care. As long as the Divine Principle was true, everything was justified.

"What were you really doing to help anyone else with all that money you were making?"

Ray would never understand that just having people give to the Messiah was a blessing for them.

All day the first day I listened but never responded, agreed, disagreed, or expressed any opinion. I kept it all to myself. Midway through the second day, I exploded.

"What are you offering me?" I yelled. "I know what the world is like, that's why I left. All you're doing is taking something away from me." I was furious. "I want to see my parents!"

"I'm sorry, it's best if you don't see them."

"What? I just want to talk to them." I was irate.

Ray reluctantly agreed that I could briefly speak with them. He left the room and my parents came in. I hadn't seen my dad since the van ride, and I hadn't seen my mom at all. They sat down on the two folding chairs next to my bed.

"I'll make a deal with you," I said. "I'll listen to Ray for five days. After that, I get to choose what I want to do."

"We're sorry, it's not up to us," my dad apologetically replied.

"What do you mean it's not up to you?" My dad was *always* in charge.

"It's up to Ray and the other guys. When we hired them, they said we had to do it their way or not at all."

Defeated, I closed my eyes and clenched my teeth. "Just leave."

My father later told me that he and my mom initially intended to keep their promise not to have me kidnapped, but everything changed when I sent them the engagement photo of me and Jim. They were afraid that if I married this stranger, I'd be lost to them forever. My parents and sisters agreed that it was imperative I be kidnapped from the Moonies. So now, after countless hours of preparation and the many thousands of dollars my parents paid for my kidnapping and deprogramming, here we were.

For three days things continued pretty much the same, except that a mole I had on my finger for several years just fell off. I slept about fourteen hours a day. On the third day, I knew I wasn't going to get out of this, so I changed my tactics. I started pretending that I believed them. Ray went on and on with all his stuff, and I gradually started to concede. Once I became more agreeable, they let me out of my room for meals. But I noticed there weren't any knives at the table.

My father said, "I knew you'd snap out of it." The others were a little more cautious. Judy sometimes gave me back rubs at night. "How do you feel, El?" It was distressing to lie to her.

I figured that after a while they'd let me go, and I'd just return to the church. But even after I started pretending that I believed them, they kept up our daily deprogramming sessions. One day Ray took out a tape recorder.

"Did you know Dina and May?" he asked.

"Yeah." Of course I knew Dina. She was my first group leader, and I adored her. May also had been on staff at Boonville and played clarinet in the band. I also knew they both had been deprogrammed several years earlier and never came back to the church.

"I've got a tape recording of them. Do you want to hear it?"

No, I didn't want to hear it, but what could I say? "Sure."

On the recording they both talked about how they'd been deceived into joining the church, how they made tens of thousands of dollars, yet it never went to help anyone.

Dina and May had been deeply dedicated leaders, so their words were quite unsettling. In fact, of everything Ray had shared with me so far, Dina and May's testimony was the first thing that put a chink in my armored wall, though I wasn't ready to admit it.

Our entire group—five bodyguards, two deprogrammers, my parents, Judy, and myself—stayed at this remote Texas farmhouse for ten days. Since I pretended to agree with them for the last few days we were there, I thought I'd be free to go. But at the end of the ten days, they said they were taking me to a cult rehabilitation center. I wasn't done yet.

Several of the bodyguards, my parents, Judy, and I flew to Ohio and then drove to the rehabilitation center. Later I found out that my parents came along because they couldn't go home. There was a warrant out for their arrest, initiated by the Moonies. My parents had kidnapped me against my will, which was illegal.

The rural rehabilitation center had formerly been a modest resort of sorts, perhaps a family camp. Ten cabins of varying sizes surrounded a large swimming pool, but since it was November, the water in the pool was frozen. Judy and I shared a cabin with two bedrooms, a small living room, and a tiny kitchen. That was really tough because she kept probing me, asking me what I was thinking. I couldn't tell her the truth. I didn't trust her or anyone. I tried talking about as many positive things as I could about the church, while also appearing that I was glad I was out. I hated lying to her, but I had no choice.

A few other people were living at the rehabilitation center, but they were all staff. I was the only "client" when I arrived. Jeff, one of the bodyguards, lived with his wife in the cabin next door. Jeff initially seemed like a big, burly thug, but he turned out to be a big, burly, sweet, down-home guy. Redford, who ran the rehabilitation center, lived in a larger cabin a few doors down from us with his wife and children. Then there was John, a counselor who had been in the Moonies, and Lou, who'd been in the Hare Krishnas.

Redford reminded me of the actor Robert Duvall. A rugged cowboy with a receding hairline and a deep heart, he was the only person I felt I could consider trusting with any emotional intimacy. Although I wasn't yet ready to reveal anything, Redford had enough depth and compassion that I would consider it. As far as the other "counselors" went, I wouldn't trust them with a thing.

There wasn't much to do at the rehab facility, and the weather was brutal. With the wind chill factor, the temperature got down to seventeen degrees below zero. My first excursion was to the mall to buy some winter clothes. The only clothes I had were the skirt, blouse, and sandals I was wearing when they kidnapped me on a warm Houston day, plus the nightgown and bathrobe my mom had brought. I went to the mall with Redford and my parents. I picked out some clothes, then stopped in the art store. When I asked my parents if I could have some paints, my dad got tears in his eyes.

"Of course, pick out anything you want."

I selected seven tubes of acrylic paint, a few brushes, and some paper.

A few days later the warrant for my parents' arrest was dropped, and they went home.

Redford and I went for a run most mornings. We'd run down a trail that led to an open field, which he said was a landing field. *A landing field?* I started scheming. If a plane was about to take off when we reached the field some morning, I could run to the plane, jump in, and get away.

I had other escape plans as well. There was a large window in my room. You could only open it a few inches because it was held in place by a chain. In the middle of the night, I attempted to break the chain so I could climb out the window and hitchhike to the Moonies in New York. But I was so nervous that I didn't try very hard.

My inner world swirled like a frantic wind, with branches, newspapers, and trash cans blowing in all directions and slamming into the confines of my head. Total turmoil. My doubts were mounting, but I didn't feel safe discussing them with anyone. I was still pretending that everything was fine and that I believed what they were telling me. I kept playing it cool, like I was on their side. Because what if my doubts about the church were only Satan fooling me?

What if Satan had sucked me in so far that I couldn't see clearly anymore? I was engaged to be married. Did that mean if I left the church now that I'd be condemned to hell? On the other hand, what if everything I had believed for the past six years was not based on The Truth? Who could I talk to? Certainly not the deprogrammers. Nor even anyone in the church. Each side had their distinct opinions, and I no longer felt I could trust either of them. I felt increasingly isolated, confused, and tortured.

I thought back to what Norman used to say in his lecture about the coming of the Messiah. "Who can you ask if you should follow this man? Not your parents nor your friends, and certainly not your rabbi or your priest. The only one you can ask is God."

I pleaded with God. "If you can tell me anything, you must tell me this! Is Reverend Moon the Messiah?"

He didn't answer. I made up reasons for His lack of response. He's probably thinking, "After six years of studying The Truth, living this life, she should know without asking me." Like in the Bible when John the Baptist questions from prison whether Jesus is the Messiah—by then it was too late.

When I overheard Redford and Ed talking about going after two girls in Oakland, I wanted to warn them, so I wrote a note to Rebecca, my last group leader from the Oakland Family, telling her what I'd heard. This could have been my chance to ask the Moonies to rescue me, but I didn't tell her where I was. I was so confused by now that I didn't know what I wanted. One minute it seemed like all this brainwashing stuff could be true; the next moment, it seemed ludicrous.

I didn't have access to stamps, envelopes, or a mailbox, but Judy was leaving the next day, after a week's stay with me, and I was going with her to the airport. I folded up the letter and wrote Rebecca's address on the outside. After we dropped Judy at her gate, I told the bodyguards that I needed to use the bathroom. In the bathroom, I left my letter on a sink, with a note saying, "Please mail this."

After Judy left, I still had a constant chaperone. Jeff, my main bodyguard, slept in my cabin at night. When he left early each morning, he'd lock my cabin door so I couldn't sneak away. As time went on, I saw more and more contradictions in the church but still clung tightly to the Divine Principle. There was no way to sort through the validity of everything I'd learned in the Moonies, but I figured that if the Divine Principle was The Truth, that justified everything else. But I was afraid to honestly examine the Divine Principle.

A little while after Judy left, several of the staff and I took a trip to Pittsburgh. We went to a pizza parlor to hear live music by a guy who previously had been in the Divine Light

Mission cult. I'd been scheming all week. During dinner I would go to the bathroom and climb out the window. Then I'd hitchhike to New York where I could hook up with The Family again.

Several parents of ex-cult members met us at the restaurant. They all raved about how wonderful I looked, noting that I didn't appear to be "floating" or spaced out. While they complimented me, I was thinking, *How am I going to get out of here?* I noticed there was a door across from the bathroom that led outside, so if I couldn't get out the window, at least I could run out the door.

Toward the end of dinner, I excused myself. Just before entering the bathroom, I glanced back and saw Redford and John watching me. Sweating and nervous, I went inside. Damn, there was no window. I'd barely been in there a minute when someone knocked on the door. Shit! There was no way I could escape now. Defeated but also relieved, I came out and returned to the table as if nothing had happened.

A few days later, I was allowed to call Daniel, the church leader in Oakland whom I used to have a crush on and who had once been my chaperone during a trip home to see my family. He had left the church two years prior. What a relief to talk to him. I could finally let down my guard. It was the first somewhat honest conversation I'd had in over a month. Daniel didn't position himself on one side or the other of the Moonie debate. He claimed that he had simply walked away with no recriminations against the church and that his relationship with God had grown while he was a Moonie. Prior to my conversation with Daniel, everyone else I knew who had left the church had switched sides and become its enemy. Those black-or-white positions vexed me.

Meanwhile, John, Jeff, Redford, and I continued our nearly daily meetings to discuss various aspects of cults. I often felt edgy during our meetings. When we gathered to talk about mind control, I was emotional and irritated. I didn't feel completely safe with John or Jeff. I only wanted to talk to Redford.

I finally asked Redford if I could speak with him privately. We went to his office, but once we were alone, I wasn't sure what I wanted to say. My whole body was rigid with tension, then I started shaking. I broke out into a sweat, and next thing I knew I was shivering with chills. I wished Redford would hold my hand, but I was afraid to ask him. Turned out, I didn't have to. Redford took my hand, and I squeezed his hand so hard that it turned white. I felt like I was holding on for my life.

The voices in my head battled it out. One scowled, "Don't love me, I don't trust anyone," while the other anguished, "Please don't leave me, don't ever let go of my hand." Trembling with apprehension, I told him what the voices said. What I didn't say is that I was still pretending—pretending that they had convinced me and pretending that I had dropped my allegiance to the church.

Exactly one month to the day after I was kidnapped, I sat on my bed, locked in my room, and decided I had two options. Either talk to someone here with complete honesty or flip out. I simply couldn't hold on anymore.

I went to Redford's office and knocked on the door.

"Hello, Ellen. Come in, have a seat." He pulled out a chair for me, and we both sat at his small round table.

"I have to talk to you." I took a deep breath and went on. "I have just been pretending to believe you. I am not convinced that the church is wrong. I can't hold this inside any longer."

I waited for his shocked response.

With a calm smile, Redford momentarily rested his hand on mine. "That's okay. I figured you were faking it."

"What? You did? How did you know?"

"The biggest clue was that you never complained about Jeff. You've been too accommodating and accepting of having a bodyguard."

I couldn't believe it. What a thing to give it away. Finally, I didn't have to lie anymore. Relief flooded through me.

"Well, I didn't say I believe you now. I just said I'm unsure."

"That's fine. What else do you need to know to help you decide?"

"I still think the Divine Principle is true. If it is, that justifies everything else. If it's not, then everything falls apart. So, I need to study the Divine Principle. Maybe compare it to the Bible since in the lectures at the farm they used the Bible to prove the veracity of the Principle."

"Okay. Why don't we set up a study session for you with John. He knows the Divine Principle, and he could help you go through it."

I grinned. Previously I'd considered John an incompetent irritant, but now that I was willing to honestly look at this stuff, I didn't mind working with him.

Back in my room I took out a piece of paper, a ballpoint pen, and a magazine to write on. Then I settled into a chair. I was ready to make a list of questions that John and I could research together. I figured I had a bunch of them waiting to be exposed, now that I was willing to take a close look. I thought they'd jump out, shiny and precise. But it was more like walking down a country road on a foggy day. Was that a question in the distance? While I'd been clenching my fist around my steadfast faith in the Divine Principle, my conviction had actually been quietly leaking away.

John and I sat in the kitchen of the main cabin with the Bible and the Divine Principle on the table side by side. He pointed out contradictions. At this point I hardly cared what they were, I was almost looking for an excuse to finally let go. When I found one that tipped the scale, my resistance crumbled, and I exhaled with relief.

I didn't have to cozy up to one more stranger with the hidden intention of recruiting them. I didn't have to sneak into one more office building, lugging around my huge bundle of flowers while avoiding the security guards. I didn't have to drag myself out of my sleeping bag every day, after only four hours of sleep. And I didn't have to marry Jim.

After three months at the cult rehab center, I was free to go. With not a penny to my name, I returned to Los Angeles and moved back in with my parents.

I would soon discover that going through deprogramming was just the beginning. Building a new life was far more difficult.

Act Three

The Rest of My Life

(1981–2019)

Los Angeles
(1981–1985)

16

So, This Is Freedom?

This is the last chapter Eliana drafted before receiving the diagnosis of terminal cancer, and she set it in the present tense to invite readers even more directly into her internal world as she struggled to create a new life after the Moonies. The subsequent chapters are equally intimate (although the verb tense varies to preserve the integrity of each individual poem, short story, letter, and reflection), which was Eliana's expressed desire when she turned over her private journals to me (Stacey Stern). To honor another wish of Eliana's, I finished writing her memoir by culling and adapting her vast collection of personal writings and developing additional material based on conversations we had during the final months of her life.

* * *

I feel defeated. For the past six years, I thought I was the savior. I was going to save my parents and my sisters. I was going to bring them to the Messiah. I had been chosen to save the world. As it turned out, my family had to save me.

How can I ever trust my feelings again? Do feelings have anything to do with what's actually true? I never cried at the rehab facility, but now that I am back in LA, I am drowning in grief. Everything I believed in has been yanked out from under me. My community is gone, but even more devastating, I have no purpose or meaning. I had been so proud of the person I forced myself to become in the Moonies, especially my courage, creativity, and chutzpah. Now I have zero confidence, especially in social situations.

After living with my parents for a few months, I moved into my own apartment. Although I've begun taking classes at a community college, I avoid interacting with my classmates and barely speak to anyone. Except my therapist. And I talk to her nearly every day.

God is nowhere. How can that be? If the connection I experienced with God while I was a Moonie had been real, the context shouldn't matter, should it? Which part of our connection was real, and which was merely a story I invented for myself? What does "real" even mean?

Having believed that spiritual experiences pointed the way to the truth, since I first encountered God while I was in Boonville, I figured that God lived with the Moonies. Not that no one else had a connection to God, but we were in on The Truth.

Now that I live in an apartment in Santa Monica, I frequently ride my bike to the Rose Café, which is just two blocks from the beach. Cappuccinos and croissants came into style while I was gone, and the Rose Café is a hip place with good coffee and great chocolate croissants. As a

Moonie, I was delighted if I got real cream in my coffee, much less a fancy coffee drink. And even then, I didn't have money, so I'd have to barter for it with a rose.

Now here I am in the Rose Café. Legally. I didn't sneak in, and I didn't have to trade flowers for my food. Lounging on the outdoor patio, soothed by the salty smell of the ocean and the sun on my back, I bask in relief. No need to jump out of my seat and witness to every person who passes by. The world is no longer counting on me for its survival.

The next day I curl up in fetal position on my couch in my dark apartment, clutching a pillow to my stomach. I am devastated. Years lost, innocence lost, friends lost, but most painfully, my purpose is lost. I am dangling without direction. I wail in grief and squeeze the pillow desperately, fighting the urge to end it all. Having the world count on you has its pros and cons.

Many spiritual traditions talk about the value of leaving your home and everything you know. I did that for the first time when I entered the Moonies, and I was forced to do it again when I was ripped from the cult. For most people, beliefs start stacking up pretty much from the day we're born, so by the time we reach adulthood, it's hard to see the bottom layer.

But at the age of twenty-seven, I am starting over with a slate that has been wiped clean. I know all too well the consequences of building my life on a faulty premise. Everything made sense when I believed that Reverend Moon was the Messiah. Now that this foundation has been dismantled, nothing makes sense anymore.

17

Looking for My Friend

Is there anyone here whose name is God?
I am looking for my friend
my home
the one who makes dreams come true.

Once I thought I knew Him so well.
We were the best of buddies.
When I was lonely
we could embrace our tears together.

He wrote me love letters
in the fragrance of a rose.
And kissed me
through velvet petals.

He told me he would always be true.
He would never leave me.
But I can't seem to find Him now.
"God, were you ever really there?"

18

Similarities Between God and My Dad

They're both men.
They both love me.
They both make promises they can't keep.

They both tell me I'm great,
then accuse me of being bad.
(The accusations are a little different.
God accuses me of being bad,
and my dad accuses me of being wrong or weak.)

They both make me feel very guilty
for not appreciating their generosity.
They both act like they're there for me,
but don't come through.

They both emphasize the importance of relationships.
They both act like they're always right.
They both tell me I should trust them,
but don't come through.

They both inspire me to love them
and hate them.
They're both inconsistent about listening.
Sometimes they listen well,
and sometimes not at all.

19

Sweet Inspiration

I still believe You made the little bubbles on top
of my cup of coffee in rainbow colors.
And You made bran muffins to come in rich brown colors
and their smell to hold me in a trance
and their warmth to make the butter quietly disappear,
its soft yellow melting into the golden brown,
leaving the crumbly surface glistening.
I believe You made cream brilliant white
so I could watch it dance in spirals
as I pour it carefully into my deep-brown coffee.

Even though there is pain enough
to make me want to give up sometimes,
I believe You made me
to find peaceful joy
in dipping my bran muffin
in my coffee.

20

Double Room with a Bath

I dreamed that I called a hotel to book a room.
The owner said, "A double room with a bath costs such and such.
Without the bath, it's this much …
Without the something else, it's this much …"

He continued on
until I was paying the same price
but getting nothing.

With God
I feel like He's given me
let's say
ten ways to suffer.

Then He provides relief from one of the pains
and expects me to be grateful
because now I'm only suffering in nine ways
instead of ten.
Why should I have ten to begin with?

21

Everything Is Golden

My eyes open, and for a moment everything is golden. No, better than golden. Deep and rich, textured and layered, mysterious and beautiful. My heart aches. I brush my hand tenderly over the wrinkles in my blanket. The folds make patterns of dark and light. I caress them like a lover's face.

Awe pushes against the boundaries of my heart. I have to leave my apartment soon and want to take these precious feelings with me. I try to stuff my pockets with the intense love I feel. It's too big for the everyday world. I am afraid that when I walk out my door, I'll lose these feelings, and the world will look dry and mundane again.

I try to take too much of this goodness with me, and it spills all over the floor. I return to the world empty-handed and filled with pain. The outside world is so far from the one I was just in. Actually, it's the same world, but I am so far away from the person I just was.

It feels like God is taunting me, showing me something so intensely beautiful, then taking it away, as if to say, "Here's what you can't have."

I yell out, "What's the point of transporting me with a few moments of deep communion?"

No reply.

"If this is how it's going to be, I don't want any more golden moments. Same goes for epiphanies. If epiphanies have no impact on my real life, if the revelations quickly deflate in the aftermath, then you can keep your lightning bolts of inspiration."

22

A Not-So-Chance Meeting

The American Psychiatric Association held a national conference on cults in Los Angeles in 1982. When a bigwig cult researcher from UCLA dropped out at the last minute, I was asked to fill in as a guest speaker, a real live ex-cult survivor. Although I was nervous, I was glad to be chosen because I knew I had valuable perspectives to offer. About two hundred people, mostly psychotherapists and concerned parents of cult members, would be attending the conference. In contrast to the horror stories they typically heard, I would be honest, sharing both the good and the bad. I refused to exchange one kind of fanaticism for another.

As I told my story and began feeling safe with the audience, I revealed some of my more vulnerable feelings. "While I was in the Moonies, for the first time in my life, I felt like my life had purpose and meaning. We were going to save the world. But when I left, I lost everything. I no longer had a reason to live."

I spoke for nearly an hour, and when I was done, the audience clapped enthusiastically. I was their prodigal daughter who had come home. Afterward, I mingled with attendees. As I moved through the crowd, I noticed a tall, stately woman who was facing away from me. Her hair was pulled up in a French twist that showed off her long, elegant neck. When she turned to the side, I realized it was Catherine! The same Catherine I initially idealized when I was a Moonie. The same Catherine whose feet I massaged late one night in our house in San Francisco.

I suspected she wasn't attending the event as a fellow ex-cult member; rather, she likely had come to see what the enemy was up to. Even though I now was the enemy, I couldn't help wanting to put my arms around her and hug her. Approaching her from behind, I gently tapped on her shoulder. When she turned around, her expression became stiff and cold.

"Hello, Catherine. It's nice to see you. How have you been?" I asked, losing confidence.

"Very good," she said in a tight voice, as she folded her arms across her chest. "We're bringing in a lot of new members, and we've started several new businesses that are doing quite well."

Then she softened her tone and relaxed her stance. Her voice sounded concerned. "Sounds like you've been having a lot of trouble since you left."

I knew she thought I was a traitor and that my anguish was God's punishment. Still, the tenderness in her voice drew me in.

"I can understand why you left," she continued. "You always were weak in your faith."

Ouch. I wasn't prepared for that. Her verbal dagger almost cut a deadly wound. But after an initial jolt of pain, the dagger evaporated. I realized her cold manner stemmed not from righteousness but from fear. With a mix of sadness and victory, I smiled, hugged her, and walked away.

23

Exodus

I'm parting the red sea,
running from the demons that enslave me.

I'm parting the red sea
with a slow, deep slice
that cuts through my veins.

As my flesh separates,
crimson blood breaks free
like a mad dog who's been caged for too long.

I'm parting the red sea,
just a thin line between life and death.

God must have marked my parents' door,
cursing their third child
with eternal longing,
eternal frustration,
eternal rage.

I'm crossing the red sea.
Will I find peace in the land of Canaan?
Will I find peace on the other side?

Boulder

(1985–1988)

24

Move to Boulder

Longing for a change, in 1985 at the age of thirty-one, Eliana moved to Boulder. She had been working toward a bachelor's degree in psychology at UCLA, and she decided to complete her undergraduate studies at the University of Colorado. After renting a place for a year, her parents helped her buy her first house.

* * *

I bought my house because of the shelf in the master bedroom. It was made from alder, a sensuous blond wood with beautiful waves and ripples in the grain. The shelf ran the length of one wall, starting out about three feet deep before curving into a narrower strip. I'd never seen a curved shelf, and I liked the uniqueness, the color, the texture, and the form. The rest of the house was nice too, but it was the shelf that sold me. I had a bed made to match the shelf, with the same type of wood and soft flowing form.

Sometimes when I was feeling depressed, I'd go to fabric stores to look at the wool tweeds and plaids. I found the colors and textures soothing. It wasn't just a mental thing, it was visceral as well. Messy, dingy, sterile environments agitated me, while aesthetic, clean, colorful environments soothed me. That's the main reason I moved from LA to Boulder. Clean, crisp, gorgeous Colorado fed my soul.

I decorated my home in soft blues, purples, and rose. Nothing fancy, rather simple and cozy. My house wasn't my mansion. It was my sanctuary. I spent a lot of time curled up on the overstuffed chair in the living room, a ficus tree hovering above my head. After placing my books, journal, and special pen on the end table to my left, and with my cup of tea and homemade banana bread on the coffee table in front of me, I'd read for hours—books like *The Tao of Physics* or articles by Carl Jung. I examined my own psyche by writing poems or imaginary dialogues with anthropomorphized aspects of myself. Sometimes my housemate invited me to go out for a beer with her and some friends, but I usually declined. I wasn't comfortable in groups or with small talk.

I didn't know how to have fun anymore. Then I met Tom while volunteering at a homeless shelter. After struggling to heal my aching heart and soul for quite some time but getting nowhere, I had decided to try offering comfort to others. Both Tom and I volunteered on Friday nights, which said something about our social lives.

I enjoyed the time we spent together at the shelter, and he seemed simple, innocent, and non-threatening—definitely not the kind of guy I would fall in love with. He was a little taller than me, had a full brown beard, and wore heavy work boots. He worked as a welder, which evoked nothing for me except blue-collar. Although most of my friends were not yet established professionals, they were going to be, or at least their parents were—white-collar was my norm. I was intrigued that Tom came from a different world.

The first time he asked me out, it didn't even cross my mind that he had romantic intentions. We went cross-country skiing at Eldora Mountain Resort, then he took me to a cozy Italian restaurant tucked away in the mountain town of Nederland. It was unusual for me to spend an entire day with someone because I'd typically get anxious after a few hours and want to go home and be by myself.

I was surprised that when we got back to my house and Tom asked if I wanted to go to a movie, although I was exhausted, I said yes. I told him I wanted to take a hot bath first, but if he didn't mind, he could hang out in the living room and read a magazine. The hot bath was not to get clean; it was my way of taking some space, recuperating, and transitioning into the next activity. I could let go in scheduled periods of time, then I'd need to take control again.

Tom drove a 1954 deep-red pickup truck. The interior was a bit shabby, but the exterior was in beautiful condition. As we drove to the movie, I sat to the far right. When he said, "You can sit closer to me," I realized we were on a date.

A couple days later, he invited me over for dinner. He was learning to play the flute, and after dinner he played me a love song. His vulnerability was touching. I didn't know any other grown man who would play an instrument for someone after only a couple of lessons, much less a love song. On our next date, he brought me a flower made out of iron, which he had forged himself. The thought was sweet, but the flower was dreadfully clunky.

Soon I was spending every weekend with Tom in his converted barn in Gold Hill—a small, picturesque mountain town, with a historic general store and an original stagecoach stop that had been converted into the local bar. It was a real town, not just a tourist destination, with two good restaurants and health food in the general store.

On weekdays I would contemplate the meaning of life, and on weekends I would play mountain woman. I embraced it so wholeheartedly because I knew it wouldn't last. Tom told me that the moment he fell in love with me was during a backpacking trip in the Wind River Range in Wyoming. We were fishing at a lake, and when I caught a fish I said, "Let me break the fish's neck. If I'm going to eat it, I should be able to do the dirty work."

Though I can't say I was in love with Tom, I loved what he did for me. He liberated the woman who wanted to break the fish's neck and the woman who wanted to get back out into the world and play. Without Tom, I would have spent every day sitting on my overstuffed chair, reading Jung while trying to decipher the influence of the collective unconscious on my life and the meaning of the previous night's dream.

Tom didn't enjoy working as a welder under the direction of others. He dreamed of owning a blacksmith shop where he could make his own hand-forged creations. When he was offered a job in a blacksmith shop near the ritzy town of Vail, known for its fine ironwork, he accepted the offer, figuring it would bring him one step closer to opening his own shop. His new home in Minturn was about two hours away from Boulder, so it took more of an effort to see each other. I didn't mind the drive, though. I would listen to a book on tape and get thoroughly engrossed in some mystery while driving along gorgeous mountain roads.

The week before Valentine's Day, Tom said he wanted to take me on a surprise adventure for the holiday weekend and that I should pack warm clothes in my backpack and bring my cross-country skis. The last time someone had done something for me on Valentine's Day was in third grade, when all the kids passed out cards to everyone in the class. Needless to say, I was thrilled.

When Tom picked me up in Boulder that Friday afternoon, we drove up the canyon past the town of Ward, then down the highway before pulling over on the side of the road.

"Here we are."

"This is it? This is the surprise? Where are we going?"

"You'll find out. Get your stuff. We'll put our skis on by that gate." He pointed to a gate that looked like it was the beginning of a road or driveway. The snow was deeper over there, deep enough to ski.

We put on our backpacks and carried our skis to the gate. He took a key out of his pocket, opened the gate, and we walked through. Then he locked it behind us.

"Ready?"

"I guess so, since I don't know where we are or where we're going."

"Don't worry, just follow me."

We started out skiing along the road, then picked up a small trail into the woods.

"I hope this is right," Tom said hesitantly.

"Don't get me lost in here."

We came to a slight decline, and Tom led the way.

"Whoa!" he shouted as he collided into low-hanging branches and fell over. He turned around and called back to me, "Be careful. The weight from the backpack makes you go faster."

Tom got up, ducked under the branches, and waited for me on the other side.

"Yikes!" I yelled, as I crashed into the tree.

We spent the next twenty minutes discussing the laws of physics as we continued to ski deeper into the woods. "Does the weight of the backpack really make you go faster, or does it just feel like you're going faster because you're whacked out of balance?"

When we entered a small clearing, Tom said, "Look up."

I looked at the sky and didn't notice anything. I looked around at the trees, and there, about thirty-five feet up, was a tree house.

"Oh, Tom, I can't believe it! That is so cool! Is that where we're going to stay?"

"Yep, it belongs to my buddy, and he said we could use it this weekend."

"It looks amazing."

We skied over to the tree house and took off our skis. The tree house was supported by four or five trees, with a staircase leading up to it. We climbed the stairs, Tom unlocked the front door, and we went inside.

"Oh my God, this is incredible!"

Inside were a wood-burning stove, a couch, a small table and chairs, and a sleeping loft. Attached to the front of the tree house, overlooking the clearing, was a small deck with a blue-vinyl-covered seat from a bus.

The incredible treehouse in the Colorado woods.

We cooked dinner over the wood-burning stove and ate by candlelight. This was a dream come true—a candlelit dinner in a tree house with a man who cared for me. I took Tom's hand in my own and kissed it as I whispered, "Thank you."

Tom stoked the fire before we crawled into bed. I decided in that moment that there was nothing better than lying in a warm bed next to a sweet man in the middle of the woods. I opened the window to let in fresh mountain air and snuggled closer to Tom.

"If we were to get married, how many kids would you want?" I asked. It really wasn't fair of me to ask because I had no intention of marrying him, but I was caught up in the moment.

"I'd want a boy and a girl. I'd take them fishing and camping and teach them how to live in the woods."

The fantasy was seductive. I didn't want kids, but when I was around Tom, I thought about what a great father he'd be. We'd have a simple, down-to-earth life, and Tom would love me forever. But then I'd think about the emotional depth and intense passion I was still looking for and knew I wouldn't be satisfied.

Tom pulled me close and sucked on my earlobe. My whole body tingled as I sighed with pleasure. We made love as the tree house rocked and swayed in the wind.

At midnight, silver rays of moonlight spread across the bed.

"I'm boiling hot in here," I said. Between the wood-burning stove and making love, we'd worked up quite a sweat.

"Move over, I want to see the moon." Tom crawled over me so he could look out the window. "It must be full, it's like daylight out there. But there are too many trees to know for sure."

"I can't sleep. I'm too hot and restless."

"What do you want to do?"

I thought for a moment. "Why don't we go skiing naked?"

"Yeah, sure," he replied sarcastically.

"No, I mean it. We won't go far. Just to do it."

"You really want to?"

"Yeah, come on, let's do it."

We scrambled down the loft ladder giggling like two little kids getting into mischief as we went out into the brilliant night wearing nothing but socks and ski boots. The moon cast mystical shadows across the snow. We fastened on our skis and glided into the center of the clearing. There we stood. Two naked lovers in silent devotion to the goddess moon.

25

Hopping a Freight Train

"Don't touch me, I'm all dirty."

"That's okay, I like you that way."

Tom had just come in from his job at the blacksmith shop in Vail, and his hands, T-shirt, jeans, and work boots were black with grease. But I meant it when I said I liked him that way. He was sexy in a primal way. He had the build of a man who earned his muscles through real work, not with barbells at the gym. He was just an inch taller than me, but when I stood close to him, with his beautiful muscles, tight Levi's, full beard, and worker hands, he felt like a real man.

Tom went into the bathroom to wash his hands and face, and I lay down on his bed. As I looked up at the cracked popcorn ceiling, I smiled with contentment. I hadn't seen Tom for two weeks, and it felt good to be around him. On my visits to Minturn I entered his world, which was so different from the well-ordered, refined surroundings in my Boulder home.

Tom's unmade bed was covered with an Indian print bedspread of beige, brown, red, and green. The bed tilted to one side, which may have been the cheap metal bed frame, but more likely, it was the uneven floor. This house was slapped together to provide shelter from a storm, and it barely did that, much less appeal to one's aesthetic sense. The carpet was vomit-colored browns and golds, the bedroom walls were pale yellow, and there were dull green walls in the living room. The few pieces of furniture were old but functional—a wooden dresser in the bedroom, a rocking chair and couch in the living room. The kitchen had a card table and three chairs.

Tom came in, sat on the edge of the bed, and unlaced his boots.

"What do you want to do this weekend?" he asked.

"Let's hop a freight train."

He turned around and looked at me. "Really?"

"Yeah, we've been talking about it forever, let's finally do it."

"I don't know. I'm pretty beat."

"Oh, come on. It'll be fun. We might not get another chance."

He lay down on the bed next to me. "Let me sleep for half an hour, and then we can talk about it."

When he woke up, I asked again, with guarded enthusiasm, "So, what do you think about the freight train?"

"It could be fun, but we gotta figure out when they come in and where they go."

"Do they stop here?"

"I think so. I'm sure they at least slow down when they go through the station at the end of town."

"I have an idea. Let's go down to that coffee shop by the station. The train guys probably hang out there. We could get a table and eavesdrop, and maybe they'll say something about when the trains come in."

We bundled up for the cold October night and walked arm in arm down the main street of Minturn. The town was only about five blocks long and three blocks wide in 1987, and many of the day laborers who worked in Vail lived in the shacks of Minturn.

We walked into the coffee shop and were directed by the middle-aged waitress behind the counter to "just sit anywhere." We settled into a booth by a steamy window, adjoining a booth with two guys who looked like they worked for the railroad.

"La de da, I think I'll just stretch a bit," I said as I leaned my head back to listen in on the railroad guys in the booth behind us. After a few fruitless minutes, I gave up on the incognito plan and turned my head around.

"Do you guys work on the trains?"

"Yep," they nodded.

"What time do they pull through here?" I casually inquired.

"The eastbound comes in around 6:00 a.m., and the westbound around noon."

I was almost disappointed this was so easy but decided to take advantage of the situation.

"Does anyone ever hop the freights?"

"Yeah, sometimes."

"What do you do when you find them?"

"We probably wouldn't do anything. Can't speak for the other guys though."

"Um, just wondering. Thanks."

After Tom and I finished our coffee, I smiled and nodded at the railroad men as we left the restaurant.

"Let's take the 6:00 a.m. eastbound," Tom said once we were outside. "It'll still be dark, and I know where we can hide until the train pulls in."

"Okay. I'll pack food, and we can bring a sleeping bag to cuddle in." I pressed up close against him. "I can't believe we're finally doing this."

"You seem like a giddy teenager … it's fun having an eighteen-year-old girlfriend," he said with a wink and a smile as he brushed my cheek with the back of his hand.

When we got back to his place, I packed granola, milk, orange juice, and utensils, while Tom rolled up his sleeping bag and stuffed everything into his backpack. A few hours later, we rose with excitement when the alarm clock rang at 4:30 a.m., and we got two cups of coffee at the twenty-four-hour convenience store on our stroll to the train station. Once there, we huddled on a log in a dark corner, sipping our coffee in the cold morning air. The moment felt perfectly complete. I had everything I needed—a man, a hot cup of coffee, food, a sleeping bag, and an adventure waiting to happen.

"As soon as the train comes in, I'll say go, and we'll run for it. Just follow me, I'll jump on and help you up."

"Okay." Now I was feeling butterflies in my stomach. I took deep breaths to calm my anxiety and kept checking my watch. At two minutes to six, we heard the rumblings of a train.

"Get ready," he said.

The train pulled in, slowing, slowing, until it came to a stop.

"Okay, go!"

Tom ran toward a flatbed, threw the backpack aboard, then hoisted himself up. I grabbed onto the edge of the car but was too frazzled to pull myself up. I could just see it, the train would start moving again, and my legs would get mangled under the wheels.

"Grab my hand!"

I took his hand, and he quickly pulled me on board. The car we had jumped on was a flatbed with no side walls, just a low, partial roof.

Tom gestured and quietly said, "Let's go back there so they won't see us, at least until we leave the station." We crept into the darkest corner of the flatbed and waited. We huddled there for close to an hour.

"I guess we didn't have to be in such a hurry to get on. Maybe we could have found a nicer car, a box car would have been warmer, but at least on this one we'll have a better view," I rambled.

Finally, the train started to roll. "Ooh, here we go!" My voice trembled as if we were taking off on the Matterhorn at Disneyland.

It was a gray, drizzly day, and the morning light was just breaking through. We were lying on the cold steel with a sleeping bag wrapped around us. As we left town, the sun was desperately trying to crack its way through the clouds. I propped up on my elbows to watch the narrow river wander through the wide swaths of farmland. No roads, no people, just the steady rhythm of the train passing through misty fields of green.

Warm and dry in my sleeping bag, I perched there and felt the heartbeat of the train gently rocking me through a visual dream. No thoughts, no past, no future, just the pleasure of being, of observing—intimate yet detached. I could have done this for a very long time, but I sensed Tom was uneasy.

"As soon as we slow down again, we can jump off," he suggested.

I said nothing, trying to hold on to the sweetness of this trance.

The train followed a small river, and after about two hours, the river became fast and wide. Our side of the river was expansive open fields, and on the other side, there were a few scattered houses. The train began to slow down.

"If we slow down enough, we can jump off."

"But Tom, I don't think there's anywhere to go. I haven't seen one bridge across the river or any roads. If we get off here, we might be really stuck."

The train slowed to a stop.

"I guess you're right. There's no way we can cross that river without a bridge."

The sun, now high in the sky, had persuaded the clouds to go away. The green fields were dotted with white daisies. Across the river, I could see a red tricycle abandoned on a dirt road.

We heard voices nearby and moved into a corner so as not to be seen. The two railroad workers I had talked with the night before at the coffee shop walked by.

"What do you think they're looking for?" I whispered. It obviously wasn't us because although it wasn't acknowledged, they had to know we were there. "Maybe the train's broken. What if we get stuck here for days?"

"I doubt it. Maybe they're just taking a walk."

After a few minutes of trying to hide, we gave it up and walked around on the car, stretching our legs and taking in the sun. I badly needed to pee but was afraid to risk getting off the train.

"I'm going to do it over the edge," I told Tom. "You don't know how lucky you guys are. God had no consideration for women."

Just as I was pulling my pants back up, Tom urgently whispered, "Hey, someone's coming."

A man jumped from the next car onto ours. He had long, greasy hair and wore a tie-dye T-shirt.

"Hey man, how ya doin'?" Tom called.

"Not bad. You've got a nice car here. I've been hanging on to a ladder for most of the ride."

I walked over and greeted our guest. I reached out to shake his hand and immediately regretted it. His fingernails were about an inch long, his hands were grimy, and he smelled awful.

"Where are you going?" I asked.

"To Denver, to the Grateful Dead concert."

"This train isn't going to Denver."

"It's not?"

"No, you must have taken the wrong one."

"Where does it go?"

"Pueblo's the last stop."

"Guess I'll just hop another train from Pueblo."

"We've got some food. Do you want something?" I offered.

"No, just thought I'd take a walk."

The train started to move again. "Better go now," he said, as he headed back in the direction he'd come from.

When he was gone, Tom and I looked at each other. "That guy was loony," he said.

"I know. He gave me the creeps. Did you see those fingernails? They were gross. I was worried he might want to stay here."

The train continued to follow the river as the terrain on both sides rose up around us. Suddenly we were at the bottom of a deep canyon.

"Oh cool!" Tom cried. "We're entering the Royal Gorge. This is incredible—our own private tour of the Royal Gorge!"

We passed under a bridge, and I looked up at the tiny people admiring their view of the spectacular scenery. But their view was nothing compared to ours. I felt like we were cheating and getting away with it—you should have to pay a fortune for this ride along the river. The train moved deeper into the canyon. No roads, no people, nothing but the wild river, the towering cliffs, and then the thundering train. Tom pulled me close, and our bodies undulated to the loping rhythm of the iron horse.

Six hours after leaving Minturn, we approached Pueblo, the end of the line.

"We're almost there," Tom said. "We better get off before we pull into the station. They could take us to jail if they find us. We're going to have to jump while it's still moving."

I had visions of calling my mother and saying, "Hi Mom. My leg got run over by a train." I wasn't sure if I was more scared of losing a limb or of what my mother would say.

When the train blew its whistle and slowed to a crawl, Tom yelled, "Jump!"

I held my breath, clenched my teeth, and jumped. I landed hard, fell forward, and put out my hands to stop my fall. The gravel scraped my palms, but all my limbs were intact. I brushed myself off and wanted to cry with relief.

As we walked toward town, it started raining again. Lightly at first, but then it began to pour. When we spotted the neon sign for a Mexican restaurant, neither of us hesitated. It was a funky-looking place, the kind guaranteed to have cheap, authentic, delicious food.

Once inside we collapsed into a booth, Tom on one side of the table and me on the other. The smell of warm corn tortillas permeated the air. I swooned at the thought of a hot plate of cheese enchiladas and refried beans. Hopefully the skies would clear by the time we finished lunch. All we both wanted was to crawl into Tom's warm bed, but it was two hundred miles away.

When we left the restaurant, it was only drizzling. Tired and bedraggled, we made our way to the freeway entrance and stuck out our thumbs. Six hours to Pueblo, four hours home, and a story for the rest of my life.

San Diego
(1988–1996)

26

Letter to God

After Eliana graduated from the University of Colorado, she decided she wanted to create educational software and heard about a master's program in educational technology at San Diego State University. In the fall of 1988, she moved to San Diego (and later Del Mar). Things got darker again for her there. This is a letter Eliana wrote to God shortly after returning to California.

* * *

Dear God,

How do I express who I am? I want some way to make all the love I feel tangible. It's not enough to feel it as a fleeting experience. I want to create something with it. My love for you is so strong. But I am afraid if I love you too much, you will abandon me again and my heart will be too open to all the ugliness in this world.

I can see the perfect way you put the world together. Then I hear about eighth-grade children bringing guns to school,

225

and I can't stand it. It hurts too much to see how far we've strayed from your original vision. I can't heal it all. Since I don't know what to do, I close my heart. Maybe I blame you because I don't understand.

I tiptoe around my emotions. When I feel anger rising, I rein it in by tensing my body and moving slowly and with more control. I try to avoid thinking about volatile issues. But the more distance I create, the less I feel. Then this terrifies me, so I respond by stirring up anger. I throw a tantrum in my mind to make sure I don't fall asleep.

Everything gets so messy. Then the accuser comes in and smothers me. Anger pulls me out of numbness and confusion. But the accuser kills everything.

— El

27

Nobody Knows

Thoughts of death
hum like low-level static
through every day
and every night.

I can distract myself
for hours at a time
so that the intrusions
are barely audible.

But at the end of the day
when my strength is low
I break down
and cry.

Not so much because of
the tormenting thoughts
but because
nobody knows.

28

Playing with Knives

I stood in the kitchen holding a carton of Häagen-Dazs ice cream. Sometimes chocolate made the pain go away. But it had to be bittersweet chocolate, intense and rich.

Frustration stormed out of me without warning. I threw the spoon in the sink, shoved the ice cream back in the freezer, and grabbed a knife from the drawer in front of me. I took the big one, the one drenched with fantasies of suicide.

I held the knife in one hand and slowly turned over my other hand. Veins made thick blue lines across the top. My life ran through there and could be stopped there.

My heart was pounding loudly, but not too fast. I placed my empty hand on the counter, clenched the knife in the other, and closed my eyes.

"Go ahead, just chop off the end of your finger."

"No, don't do that. You know it's not going to change anything."

"Maybe it will. Just try it. Or slice one of those fat veins on the top of your hand."

"That's not rational! Put down the knife and go do something constructive."

"Rational?! Constructive?! That's what you've been trying to do your whole life and look where it's gotten you. Try something else for a change."

I opened my eyes and reexamined the lines on my hand, the shadows and textures. I felt the beauty and mystery of the blood pulsing though my veins. I picked the knife back up and gently pressed the blade into my finger. Nothing happened. I dragged it lightly across my arm. Nothing happened. I put down the knife in defeat.

I walked into the living room and dropped into a chair. There was a plate on the table next to me. I picked up the plate and threw it against the wall.

"You're sick. That's not normal behavior."

I smiled.

29

Freedom of Choice

Sometimes it's hard to do what you want because there's too much freedom in that. It requires thinking about every choice, and if the only criterion is, *Do I want to do this?* then it's difficult to choose.

I need a balance of choice and freedom. It's so hard to know when to break the rules. I often have wondered why I can be so stubborn. There is usually a window during which I could go one way or the other about doing something, but then at some point, I suddenly become adamant that I won't do it.

I just realized why. I hate the conflict of indecision. When it comes right down to it, there are very few choices that have no conflict. If I think about everything I do, I can find some resistance to almost anything.

The problem is thinking.

30

Limitation

What does God, the Infinite, not have?
Limitation.

We cannot exist without limitation.
If everything is infinite, there is no separation.
There is no choice.
There is only choice with limitation.

We stand with one foot in chaos
and one foot in order.
Too much chaos,
we can't get anything done.
Too much order,
life is boring.

31

The Razor Blade

Jack had been my psychotherapist for the past three years. His office was in a cottage behind his large, beautiful Spanish-style home with arched doorways and thick stucco walls. On this particular spring afternoon, I lifted the latch on the gate that led to the path to Jack's office. A cement bench had been placed against the weathered wood fence, but I preferred to stand on the grass and gaze at the bougainvillea that climbed up the house. Massive clusters of magenta flowers next to clusters of bright orange were stunning against the white stucco wall. The brilliant colors trailed from the wall across the trellis that connected the house to Jack's office.

Jack kept fifteen minutes between clients, and his previous client had already left. When Jack opened his office door, I ambled across the grass and made my way inside and onto the couch. Once seated, I paused before removing my shoes. Then I unfolded the green-and-white woven blanket and draped it over my lap. My barrier, my protection. As always, I took my time. I never dove right in. I needed a few moments to fully arrive.

Once settled, I surreptitiously removed a razor blade from my purse and clutched it in my fist. Not so hard that it cut me, just hard enough to provide comfort.

"I brought a razor blade with me today."

I opened my fist and showed the blade to Jack.

He didn't get nervous, at least as far as I could tell. If he did, he kept it well hidden. He had enough confidence in each of us to let things be. That's when I fell in love with him all over again.

I let the unspeakable crawl out of me. I let the terror rise to the surface as I poured out my feelings. It's strange how you can hide emotions for so long, and when you're ready to let them out, they appear to be beyond your control. But when it's time to put them away again, you realize you *do* have control.

What do they do the rest of the time while they hide beneath the surface? They're not silent, I know that. I may appear to keep my feelings under control, but they keep me under their control as well.

I am ready to let my fears, emotions, and desires out into the light. I have come to love them. I love their convoluted nature. I love their mystery, their fragrance, and most of all, their power. They have fire inside. They have guts and gore. They contain strength and passion, and that's where love lives. Love doesn't live in safety and comfort. It needs conflict to grow. Like a pearl, the irritation creates something of mysterious beauty. Clean and smooth.

32

White Heat

I am white heat.
Piercing with a glare from my eyes.
People turn away before my rage can scorch them.

But not you.
You let it pass through you
because you know that the source of my rage is sadness
and that the passion of anger contains the passion of love.

I don't hate the world because I'm mean.
I hate the world because I'm soft and scared.

And I love you
because you let me hate the world
and be soft and scared
and hate you
and wish you would hold me close forever.

33

Some Days It Gets So Crowded in Here

Some days it gets so crowded in here that I have to leave. The battles continue, but I check out. It's easier to fight with another person. It's easier when they have their side and you have yours. But when all the voices are in your own head, you can't walk away.

The battle usually begins with the voice of annihilation.

"You could put a bullet through your head. That would be a powerful, explosive way to go."

I fight back, "But I don't want to die."

"You could lie on the floor and slice your wrists. Watch the red blood seep into the white carpet, imprinting patterns that will never go away."

"But I don't want to die. Why do you do this to me? What do you want from me?"

"You could overdose on pills. No, that would mess up your insides. Forget that idea."

"Please just tell me, what do you want from me? I don't want to die, but you're killing me. Please stop consuming me. Let me live."

There are no safety zones, no time outs. Annihilation is always the aggressor, like an impotent man trying to prove his power.

Then suddenly, the battle ceases. All is still inside. Very quiet and still. Everything is muted. I hold my hands in front of me and admire these finely crafted masterpieces, capable of strength and tenderness. I gaze out my window at the layers of iridescent bark on the trees and soak up the soft reds, yellows, and purples.

I stand back from the battlefield and kiss my forearms more tenderly than my mother or a lover ever has. My lips rest on the fragile blue veins in my wrist. I close my eyes and continue kissing the soft skin up the length of my forearm.

My goodness unveils itself, and it tastes so sweet. Compassion floods my body and whispers, "I'm sorry you have to fight like this."

Then I weep the tears that slowly, very slowly, begin to heal me.

34

Cutting for Compassion

I was thinking about the first time I cut myself. I was at my house on Adams. I went into the bathroom and saw a razor blade on the shelf. I picked it up and cut my finger. I'm feeling a rush just remembering it.

Then I went into my room, sat on my bed, and cried. I felt so much compassion for myself. A tender mother inside me emerged who suddenly realized how much pain I was in. She was soothing and understanding. She held me and rocked me, without blame or accusation. She was pure compassion.

My desire to return to compassion's embrace was one of the reasons I kept cutting. But it doesn't work anymore. Cutting doesn't work. Suffering doesn't work. I have to find another way. People are sick of it, and so am I.

Where can I find the love that I seek without being manipulative? Writing helps. I can write stupid, boring stuff knowing that someday I'll write something good. I already do write some good things. Plus, I just like it. Sometimes ideas emerge that I wouldn't otherwise see. Around the corner, a new revelation might appear on the page.

Besides writing, how am I going to let go of suffering? It's in my body. My entire system is accustomed to it. Even if I release the belief that it's worthwhile to suffer, my body is patterned to hold on to suffering.

I'm going to close my eyes right now and ask my body what it wants ...

"I want compassion. I don't want someone to kick me in the butt. You've been doing that for years. I don't need that. I'll grow better with love and compassion.

"I don't want to work with people who are more deprived than I am. I want to work in an uplifting environment. I don't have to break my heart to grow or help the world. It's okay to work with other white middle-class people in a cheerful environment.

"I still say try medication. Just get me up to par. You carry me around everywhere you go. I need rest. At least put me on wheels."

35

The Big Game

I don't know why I ever agreed to play this game.
Ever since I can remember
I've wanted to quit.

I've tried hard to get the team spirit,
tried hard to throw myself into the game.
But at the end of each day
it's the same old thing.
I want to quit.

I keep hoping it will change.
Just one more year
and it will change.
My whole life I've waited
and it's still the same.

There are days that it's fun.
Even moments of ecstasy.
But underneath it all
I want to quit.

People don't like you to quit this game
especially if it's by choice.
If I quit before my time
some people would be really mad.

I don't know why.
I've played the best I could.
I'm tired
and I want to go home
and rest.

36

El Shaddai

I just got home from a few days at Mount Madonna, a retreat center in the mountains near Santa Cruz, California. I went for the Yom Kippur services led by Reb Zalman, one of the founders of the Jewish Renewal movement. Thanks to him, I'm feeling refreshed and cautiously optimistic at the moment.

Let me back up and say I was feeling really, really down before I went. A few months earlier, I gave God an ultimatum: "You have until Yom Kippur to come through. After that, I am giving up on you."

So I registered for this Yom Kippur retreat, packed up all my suffering and hoped it would blow away in the country air. I didn't want to give up on God, but I also didn't believe He could suddenly transform His nature. Could He? That would be unsettling.

I went to the retreat with my anger, a desire for change, and a yearning for revelations. I reasoned that if anything miraculous could happen, it would be more likely far from home, on sacred land.

A miracle *did* happen. Reb Zalman taught us that in Judaism God has many names, and one of them comes from Genesis, where God is called El Shaddai, which means the breasted one. I had perceived God as a harsh, judgmental king. But I love this new image of God as the breasted one— a loving, nurturing presence. A big boob in the sky!

This is the God I have longed for. I feel deep shifts within me. I think I'm truly, finally ready to stop suffering.

37

Leaving Jack

Eliana incorporated fantastical imagery in this short story.

* * *

It happened every time I left Jack's office. A lifetime of hurt ripped open a gash in my side. I pressed my left hand over the wound and placed my right hand on top, pushing hard to prevent my guts from spilling out. I walked down the street, trying not to make too much of a mess as green, murky stuff oozed through my fingers. I had to hold it in place until I got to my car.

Once in my car, I pressed on the wound even harder, as if I could push it into oblivion. The ache was sharp and deep. I grabbed my sweater and clutched it to my side, trying to stop the leakage, to cover the gaping hole, to obliterate the pain.

When I got home, I closed my eyes and paused in the hallway, indecisive. Feeling a tug from a nameless force, I went to the kitchen and pulled a long, sharp knife from the

247

wooden knife rack. Then I got in bed and crawled under the covers.

I know it sounds nuts, but the knife was like my blankie. Having it close was comforting. I held the handle with one hand and my gushing side with the other. There was a tall eucalyptus tree outside my window, and since my apartment was on the second floor, my gaze rested on her trunk and branches, far above the ground. Day after day, she stood there, soft and sturdy. When I woke up in the morning, when I took a nap in the afternoon, when I went to bed at night, she was there.

When she shed her bark, it peeled off in ribbons, then rolled into narrow tubes, leaving baby-smooth skin underneath. Every year she shed her bark, yet here I was, stuck in the same fucking skin, stuck in the same old pain. Why couldn't I let it go?

I loosened the grip on my stomach and placed the knife on the windowsill. My cat, Pooky, sat in the doorway, his posture majestic. With luxurious gray fur and a brilliant white triangle on his chest, he was the most handsome cat I had ever seen.

I had been working on a little poem and recited it to myself.

"'Twas the night before tomorrow and all through the house, only Pooky was stirring, stalking a fake mouse. My knife was placed on the windowsill with care, in hopes that death soon would be near."

"You don't have the option to die," Pooky stated with authority. "When you got me from the pound, you signed a contract stating that you would be at my beck and call for my entire life. Until then, you have to stick around."

Pooky was more complex than his name. Occasionally scary, sometimes funny, macho on the outside, tender on the inside. He walked like a ballet dancer with his paws turned out. Now he jumped up on the bed and pushed his back against my hand, triggering my automatic scratching response.

A branch from the eucalyptus tree brushed the window, and the leaves whispered, "You don't really want to die."

I opened the window so I could hear her better.

"I know it seems like a good solution, but now's not your time."

"Then what should I do?" I cried.

"You have to move on. It's time to leave him."

The tree was talking about Jack. I had been seeing Jack as my psychotherapist for six years now. And I was in love with him.

You can roll your eyes at the cliché, with transference and all, but to me, it was all-consuming. I always fell for the unattainable ones. The last love of my life was God, and that hadn't worked out so well.

Talking with Jack was sort of like talking with God. Neither of them answered me. I could pour out my heart, and Jack would just nod his head. I felt needy and trapped. I was afraid I couldn't live without him.

"You are not getting better. Every time you see him, you leave in pain. It has become an emotionally abusive relationship," said my internal voice.

A man's voice interrupted, "That's not how I see it."

The voice was unmistakably Jack's. I turned around and saw Jack sitting in his beige leather therapist's chair in the corner of my bedroom.

"I represent all the love you didn't get as a child. You need to keep seeing me until you've resolved your conflicted feelings. We are just getting started. If you leave me now, you'll never get rid of the pain."

I leaned back against my pillow. So many nights I had thought about Jack, wishing he was in bed beside me. Now that he was here in my room, my fantasy crashed into reality (or at least into another fantasy), and I wanted him gone. Far gone. Rage and power surged through my fingertips, and I zapped him out of my room.

A realization emerged. It was as if it had been lingering in the back of my mind until right now, when I was finally ready to receive it. Six years. Six years in the Moonies. Six years with Jack. This was my chance. Last time my parents had to rescue me. This time I'd rescue myself.

38

Goodbye, Old Life

I had a ceremony tonight to say goodbye to my old life. It has been a profound couple of months. Ever since I cut the dark man loose, the one that contained the belief that suffering will bring me closer to God, I feel different.

Although I'm more willing to let go of suffering, it still hangs over me. It's in my cells. I haven't known how to change that. This morning, finally, I decided to take medication. My body needs a physical change—or at least a shelf so that when I fall, I won't fall so far.

Even if the medication doesn't do anything, it is profound that I am finally, finally truly ready to release suffering. It has been an integral part of my life. I must build in replacements. I need new topics for contemplation and discussion.

What do other people talk about besides sports, food, and politics? I don't like talking about work. And I don't like hearing about other people's problems. Well, that's not entirely true, but it sure felt that way in group the other night. I am tired of dwelling on problems, other people's and my own.

I want to be able to move on even if I haven't yet convinced the world how much pain I've been in. I can't depend on the world's reaction. I may never convince group, or my mom, or my sisters of the pain I've endured.

But, for myself, I have to move on.

Return to Boulder

(1996–2019)

39

Happy Again

After eight years in the San Diego area, Eliana felt pulled to return to the majestic mountains of Boulder, where she had been happy before and hoped she could be happy again. She also started taking anti-depressants. They initially helped, but the benefits inevitably wore off. Whenever this happened, Eliana would try another medication. Then another. It took many years of trial and error—and thirty-five different medications—until Eliana found one that consistently worked well for her. She once told her sister Judy that more than a dozen years of talk therapy provided scant relief compared to the efficacy of altering her biochemistry.

* * *

I feel happy again. On my walk home, the leaves and flowers and trees were so beautiful. I was filled with gratitude for life. Usually when I feel happy, I start thinking about all the poor people who don't have anything. Then I think, "With all I've been given, I should give more to others. God wants me to be a martyr first, then be happy." But today was different. Today, I felt like my happiness *was* my gift to God. I didn't have to do anything. My appreciation was enough. This shift in perspective changes everything.

It used to be poisonous to feel good because then I'd have to save the world. On the other hand, if I didn't feel grateful, I was a bad person. It was a no-win situation.

But ever since I started picturing God as a big, nurturing boob in the sky, I have begun feeling better. The meds might be helping too.

I recently read that Rabbi Nachman said our first obligation is to feel happy. That's the most important. From there we can do other things, but happiness first.

40

Musings on Creativity and Art

Is there a difference between creating from the personality and creating from the soul? It feels like creativity that comes from the personality can be beautiful, but it wouldn't give you the shivers. Creativity from the soul is more universal, dipping into the collective unconscious.

* * *

If art is made out of conflict, I should be a great artist. Lying in bed this morning I thought, *I'm so happy.* Ten minutes later I thought, *I wish I was dead.* I guess both can be true. I don't know. That's what drives me crazy, one conflicting feeling after another. I hardly have time to feel one before a contradictory emotion intrudes.

Last night I lay on top of my bed in emotional pain. Not about anything in particular, just pain. Then I looked out the window at the beautiful trees, the shadows, the sky. It made me cry. The contrast made me cry. So much beauty and pain at the same time, it tears me apart.

* * *

I want to make art that feels like a mystery. Playful is fine and good, but mystery touches me.

* * *

I am an artist.
What is it that only I can say
in my own way?
What canvas is waiting for
the conversation
I was born to express?

I shouldn't have to
distort myself to find it.
I want the colors to
drip onto the page
even if the drips
are made from my sweat.

* * *

I am afraid to speak up
like so many women.
Maybe I have nothing worth saying.

But I step up anyway.
As I do, my courage seeps out
and into women around the world.
If they can do it, I can.
If I can do it, they can.

It's not my job to determine
how my story will touch you.
It's only my job to tell my story
by digging deep
and revealing who I am.
I am the mother of my creation.
She has her own life to lead.

* * *

The most important things in the world are nature and art.
God's creation and our creation.
Expressions of who we are.
What else is there?

41

Writing Is My Prayer

Don't forget.
Writing is my prayer.
Writing will heal.

Hold a sword over my hand
and chop my fingers off if I don't write.
God is on the edge.

Writing carries me
through confusion and pain.
I ride on the pen
and move through feelings to the other side.

I don't just write to prove I'm worthwhile.
I write to discover more of who I am.

Who am I behind the boredom?
Writing is an adventure,
but the scariest part is that nothing will happen.

I must let go of the way I think things should be.
Things are the way they are.

That's the barrier between me and God.
I want Him to make sense on my terms.
He is, or Life is, the way it is.
When I can accept that, I think I'll feel a lot better.

So, I keep writing.
God is on the edge.

42

Ellen Becomes Eliana

In 1998 Eliana legally changed her name from Ellen to Eliana.
She wrote this in 2003 in the third person about herself.

* * *

Ever since Ellen was kidnapped more than twenty years ago, she tried to talk to God. She tried to feel connected and protected. She tried to find her purpose, the meaning of her life. She wanted to be of service to the world, but some days she could hardly get out of bed. She begged for God to heal her, release her, show her the path to wholeness. But for the most part, God didn't answer.

Ellen became furious. Her God was like a withholding parent. She wondered how so many other people found pleasure and comfort in the company of God. She tried to change her concept, to see God in a new way. But the old pictures were so ingrained. She didn't know how to let go.

Finally, she was able to make the leap and take a hiatus from God. She didn't want to deny God's existence. She really didn't know if He (or She) was there or not. But Ellen wasn't going to talk to Him, count on Him, or look to Him for anything. If at some point in the future, He revealed Himself in a new way, she would consider having a relationship again.

This was a tremendous relief, and Ellen found she wasn't so angry anymore. Ellen was still talking to her healer once a week, and although she loved going to see the healer, she didn't feel much better. Ellen had tried everything—exercise, positive thinking, medication, activities, artwork, meditation, and dreamwork. She was frustrated and disappointed.

Her name, Ellen, had never felt right. Maybe a new name would provide a new start. She discovered the name she was meant to have. *Eliana*. It sounded soft and lyrical. It was Hebrew, reconnecting her to her roots. And the meaning was ironic considering that she was no longer talking to God. In Hebrew, Eliana means *My God Has Answered*.

For most of her life, she felt that God didn't answer her. But maybe He had, and she hadn't recognized the answer. With her new name, Eliana was ready for a fresh start. Yet she also wanted to revisit the things she'd loved as a child to see if they could still bring her joy.

Her first love had been making art. As a child and teenager, nothing gave her as much pleasure as creating things. She tried to rekindle that love. Eliana took classes, painted, made sculptures, and created beautiful, engaging works of art. But the process no longer excited her. In fact, she often had to force her way through. Part of her felt like art was her calling, but another part couldn't believe she'd be called to do something that didn't provide nourishment or joy.

The years went on. She had one true love, and that was her cat, Pooky. Eliana spent her happiest moments snuggling with Pooky, playing hide-and-seek with Pooky, or just watching his graceful body stretched out across the floor. Eliana knew she couldn't kill herself because she couldn't leave Pooky. No one else would care for him as well as she did.

Besides, as much as she wanted to die, there was a much stronger force aching to live. And not just to exist, but to live a big, passionate life. When Eliana got breast cancer, she wasn't surprised. She'd always thought something like this would happen. She had read that people who weren't married and didn't have a large circle of friends usually died early. That was her.

As she took a walk one day, she met a woman who read tarot cards. Eliana sat down for a reading. The woman told her she was in trouble. She had to make a clear, conscious decision. Did she want to live?

Yes, she wanted to live. Yes, she wanted to do what was needed to get rid of the cancer. Eliana was excited. Maybe this was an opportunity to face death and come back with a new enthusiasm for life.

Cancer was hard. She lost her breast. She was extremely lonely. She was nauseous and tired all the time. But cancer was nothing compared to depression. And that was an extremely valuable lesson.

Cancer would end (hopefully). People recognized it as a terrible disease and offered comfort. On the other hand, depression turned people away. They didn't know how to help. They thought they were being supportive with suggestions like, "Snap out of it, go for a run, help other people, think positive." That infuriated Eliana. Worse yet, it made her doubt herself. She wished she could snap out of it, think positive, or get rid of her depression by helping others.

Having cancer helped her view her depression differently. It confirmed and validated that the anguish she felt from depression was real. After all, it was worse than cancer.

She learned things from cancer, but the disease didn't have the transformative effect she hoped for. She trudged on. Eliana continued to try all kinds of medications to heal her depression, but none of them did the job well. *Until the thirty-fifth medication.*

The thirty-fifth medication Eliana tried actually helped. Things started to shift and open. Gradually, very gradually.

43

I Gave You Your Name

After Eliana legally changed her name, she imagined God saying this to her.

* * *

I gave you your name.
I gave you your name.
Your way is not to suffer or sacrifice.
Your way is to give love, in any way.
Make beauty.

I chose you to be here.
You are not here by accident.
I gave you your name.
You are not loving other people for only yourself,
but for me and for all your people.

Forget all the justice stuff.
Love on a simple level.
Not big.
Love your neighbors.
Make beauty.

If you remember I gave you your name,
you will know what to do.
Please tell people I love them.
It doesn't have to be the homeless or the desperate.
This is not meant to be hard.

You already have it in you,
but you don't fully believe it.
When you remember that I asked you to be here,
you will know what to do.

Rest into it.
This is not meant to be hard.
You already have it.
It's your presence.

You already have what you need.
I know that's inconceivable to you,
but it's true.
I gave you your name.

44

Grace

What if I grew up
knowing I already had
everything I need
inside me?

What if I woke up
every morning
singing
"She's got the whole world
in her hands"?

What if I sang the song
with my body?

What if I danced the song
as I made my morning oatmeal?

What if every day
I gave myself
the grace
of being who I am?

45

A Second Chance

When my mother was diagnosed with Parkinson's disease, the first thing to go was her handwriting. Her letters became jagged and illegible. Then she forgot how to use the portable phone. My dad thought that if he yelled at her enough times she'd remember. But she didn't. Then she lost interest in taking photographs and in devising treasure hunts for her grandchildren.

My sister Judy thought our mom was perfect. She thought our mom was the wisest, most compassionate woman she'd ever known. When Judy needed comfort, she turned to our mother. So when mom got sick and was no longer the person she used to be, Judy was devastated.

It was different for me. When I was little, I imagined that the lady who called herself my mother was actually a witch who had kidnapped my real mother. She wasn't an evil witch; it was just that my real mother would adore me. She would come into my room every night and sit next to me on my bed. She'd put her arms around me and make me feel safe. She would know, without me saying anything, how sad and lonely I was.

But my feelings were too big and scary for my mother. I felt I had to protect her. I had to hide my feelings or else she might collapse and die. For the next forty years, we continued to hide ourselves from each other. When she got sick, I had nothing to lose. But as her memory faded, something surprising happened. She forgot to be judgmental, and a woman I'd never known showed up.

The tension between us slipped away. It didn't matter if we had nothing to say because now we could just sit on the couch and hold hands. Or I could run my fingers through her hair or jiggle the fat under her arms.

Sometimes she'd ask for Lilly, our shared imaginary friend. Lilly was a waitress from Las Vegas whom I'd pretend to channel. I'd say, "Let me see if I can find her." Then I'd close my eyes and wait for Lilly to come through.

In my rendition of a deep southern drawl, Lilly might begin with, "Ma'am, I'm so glad to see you. It's been so long. I don't know what to say, I'm just so happy to see you."

My mom would laugh and laugh. Lilly could say things to her that I could never say. My mom absolutely adored her. My mom even found a poster of a mouse wearing a purple dress and red cowboy boots with the words, "I'm Lilly. I am the queen, and I love everything." My mother hung the poster next to her bed so she could see it every morning when she woke up.

One day as my mom lay in bed, I snuggled up next to her like I'd never done as a child. But now she was the child, with a delightful imagination. As we looked out the window at the leaves on the branches, my mother declared with glee, "Look at the elephants on the clothesline!"

I am so glad I got a second chance to love my mom.

46

Allow Beauty

Last week I was on the edge of depression, not fully immersed. I was able to keep it at bay by paying attention to things that were visually nurturing. When I noticed I was getting angry or irritable, I would look at new green leaves, clouds in the sky, or details in the flowers. It was part of my "don't think positive, think small" plan. But then I realized that's not quite right. It's more like "don't think, just look."

This is a very important distinction. Because even when I might think, "Oh, those flowers are so pretty," it wouldn't necessarily make me feel better. Sometimes it would even make me feel worse because then I'd think, "The flowers are so pretty, so why I am still so miserable?"

Then I realized the problem is the thinking. So instead, if I simply look and allow beauty to sink in, I might feel better. I practiced that a lot last week. It works best on the edge of depression. Once the depression is full-blown, I'm too far gone to go "looking" for help.

47

Vision Quest

For my fiftieth birthday, I went on a vision quest. I was hoping for dramatic insights about how to make my life more meaningful and fulfilling. I drove from my home in Boulder, Colorado, to Moab, Utah, where I met up with ten other vision quest participants and two vision quest guides. Together we drove a few hours into the mountains, then left our cars and backpacked a mile or so until we came to a lush grove of aspen trees.

This trip was half bare-bones and half luxury. We were told to bring a tarp to sleep under rather than a tent so that we'd feel immersed in nature. On the luxury side, the two guides cooked all our meals.

The vision quest was ten days in the mountains—six days of preparation to descend into the underworld, three days alone in the woods, then a final day back with the group to reintegrate and share the gifts we received during our solo. We were told we might receive a name while on our solo, so we should listen for that.

277

On day six, we dispersed from the main camp to select an area for our solo. I chose a spot nestled against a wall of rocks on one side, with an expansive view on the other side, and best of all, a small stream. We were each assigned a buddy, who was far enough away that we couldn't see or hear each other but close enough that we could arrange a system to ensure we remained safe. My buddy and I chose a specific location between our camps. Each morning, I would place a rock there. Each evening, she would leave a rock there. A missing rock would indicate that the other person needed help.

Most people fasted during their solo, but ever since I'd left the Moonies, where I had fasted more times than I care to remember, I was determined to never fast again. So when we took off for our solo, I brought protein powder to mix with stream water. Not a gourmet meal, but enough to keep me from fainting. Besides my tarp and sleeping bag, I also brought a portable outdoor shower, which consisted of a black bag I could fill with water and leave in the sun to warm. Once the sun did its job, I'd tie the bag up in a tree and enjoy a warm shower.

Since the whole point of the vision quest was to look inside ourselves, we weren't supposed to wander too far from our campsite or bring distractions such as food or reading material. On the first day of my solo, I prayed intensely for insights and revelations but had neither. The next day I decided to lighten up. I filled my black bag with water from the stream and set it in the sun. In the early afternoon when I figured the water would be nice and toasty, I tied the shower up in a tree. Then I went down to the stream, removed my clothes, and lay on a flat rock until I was also nice and toasty. Then I sat in the stream. It was a very small stream, so I couldn't fully immerse myself.

When I looked up, I saw a coyote step into the stream about twenty feet away. When he noticed me, he had a quizzical look on his face as if to say, "What are you doing here?" But he didn't stick around for me to answer.

As a kid, I loved the mud. When I was about six years old, we had a dirt area in our backyard. My mother helped me dig a hole and fill it with water. I promptly took off my clothes and got in. Here was my chance to play in the mud again. I gathered mud from the bottom of the stream and slathered it all over my body. Covered head to toe, I danced sensuously around in the sun. When I tired of dancing, I stood under my outdoor shower as the hot water washed the mud off of me. Naked in the middle of the woods, taking a hot shower, what a treat.

In that moment, I distinctly heard a voice say, "Mud Woman. That is your name."

I laughed. "Are you serious?"

"Yes, Mud Woman. That's your name."

I recalled our guide telling us that we might not receive the name we think we should. This certainly wasn't a name I would have thought of for me. But it fit.

My fierce self as revealed during my vision quest.

48

I Am Mud Woman

When Eliana inquired within about the name anointed during her vision quest, this is what she received.

* * *

Mud Woman is sensual. She is from the earth. The earth feeds her. She needs to work and play with mud. She needs mud baths. She needs to work with clay. She needs to be sensual and sexual. She needs to roll naked on the earth and in the earth. To lie on the earth. To let it soak up her pain. She needs to slither along the earth like a snake, rubbing her body on the grass.

Mud Woman is not like a tree that stands tall and waves its arms. No, she lives underground. She likes the darkness. Her gift is to show beauty in the darkness.

The shaking and stuttering she sometimes experiences are earthquakes and volcanos. There's molten fire under the surface that boils, bubbles, and explodes, altering the entire landscape. You can't ease the pressure of a volcano or earth-quake. You just have to let them crack and explode.

Mud Woman is old and wise. She has wisdom to share, but others must seek it out. She doesn't seek out others to offer her wisdom to them. They must find her.

She finds joy in quiet and in working with her hands. She loves color and texture. She loves containers. She is not spacious. It is not her job to save the world, though it is her job to bring comfort.

Mud Woman moves slowly. If she tries to move quickly, she will lose herself. Moving fast is very bad for her.

She likes dark chocolate because it is bittersweet. It is authentic. It doesn't have extra sugar to hide its bitter nature. Just enough sugar to bring out its full flavor.

She must live alone. Animals bring her comfort. Her gifts are turning mud and other raw materials into objects of meaning and beauty. Transformation. Transforming the earth. Transforming the darkness.

She is not a political warrior. Though she can be fierce and passionate, it is not her job to assume a fierce and passionate position in the world. Right now, her job is more about acceptance of her nature rather than discovering something totally new.

Pleasure is important. Pushing is not so important. She doesn't need to face the darkness; she *is* the darkness.

Mud Woman's essential features are sensuality and the need for water (emotions) to keep her alive. Without emotions she dries up, and she's no longer mud.

49

A Free Being

A free being is someone who acts according to their true self.

A free being does not cling to their identity.

A free being is not invested in how things turn out.

A free being can see clearly.

A free being is able to love others for who they really are because they don't need to manipulate them to fulfill their needs.

A free being is hard to find.

50

What I Loved on the River

Several years after her vision quest, Eliana went on a rafting trip on the Colorado River. The trip was led by two women— a writer and a sculptor. The sculptor was Native American, and she and her daughter sculpted two figures out of sand that were larger than life-size.

* * *

I loved bathing together every evening in the river. It felt like we were from another time and place, where it was customary for women to gather at the river. Some days Cathy and Gretchen would already be in the water, with their soap, towels, and shampoo laid out on the shore. Or sometimes Diane, Susan, and I would meet and scope out a good bathing spot, then the others would join us. This was the first time I had been totally naked in front of other people since I had my mastectomy.

I loved sleeping outside without a tent. The moon was full one night, and it was nearly full every other night. I loved waking up in the middle of the night when the whole camp was quiet and simply lying on my comfortable pad, gazing at the moon and stars until I fell back to sleep.

I loved peeing in the river. I don't know why that gave me such pleasure. I loved peeing over the edge of the boat or squatting on the shore. It was amazing how quickly we got used to peeing in front of one another. Without a thought, we'd pull our pants down, squat on the shore, and pee. It was so liberating.

I loved simply living in nature as a way of life. Eating and sleeping and drinking the first cup of coffee in the morning, surrounded by cliffs and sand and water.

Rita, standing on the rock with the petroglyphs on the wall in front of her and her ancestors surrounding her. Rita's gut-wrenching performance blew me away.

Rita's and Rachel's sand-sculpted lovers lying on the shore. I wanted to put my hand on the sand woman's thighs and caress them. I could have lain down next to the lovers and stayed there for hours.

Finally, our flight home. As we flew over all the places we had been, my heart was overflowing. I peered out the window, repeating, "I love you, river. I love you, rocks. I love you, sand."

51

Me, Myself, and I

I love the person who lies with me
every night.
We have known each other
since birth.
When I was small,
I cried to my mother, saying
"I hate myself."

But that little girl found her way
to self-love.
Even when I wanted to
sink into the earth and be gone,
I loved myself.

The one I lie with every night,
we like the same food.
We like the same books and movies.

I stack two fat pillows against the headboard,
my favorite place to eat dinner.
My vegetables taste better than ever before.
I am grateful to finally be home.

52

Earth, Water, Fire, Air

Earth, water, fire, air
were hanging out in the garden fair.

Swinging to the beat, having a good time
while blowing in the wind on the clothesline.

A woman came out and took in the scene,
"My laundry's dancing, what could this mean?"

Her heart fluttered open while tears filled her eyes
and this mundane moment helped her realize
that the sacredness of life isn't somewhere out there
it's stitched into the fabric of her underwear.

53

Look at Me

Look at me.
I am fabulous and flamboyant.
I am the person I was meant to be.
I'm dancing in the garden, displaying my wings.

I am part of a flock of birds, and we are flying to the moon.
We take turns leading the pack.
It's my turn tonight.
The birds fly across the deep-blue sky alongside me, and I
welcome them.

I am a swan, standing in the water displaying my
extravagant beauty.
I am quiet and peaceful, glorious and strong.

Now I am the branches above the water that rise up and shelter the swan.

Who else would like to introduce themselves?

Eye would.

The eye behind the I.

I see the world but not clearly.

I am lonely behind my new glasses.

People make fun of me, but at least I can see better than before.

I'm dancing up here.

Not waiting to be noticed.

I'm exalting in my beauty whether or not there's anyone here to acknowledge me.

54

I Am Not Depressed

I am not depressed.
I wake up and am not depressed!

Some mornings I dance and sing.
That's a miracle.
I am overflowing with gratitude.

I do have some fear that it will go away,
and I don't have the strength to be depressed again.
But mostly I'm delighted that I'm not depressed.

Does that mean I'm happy?
Yes, I feel content much of the time.
I wake up feeling fine.

Not that I jump out of bed with enthusiasm,
but I might hum a little bit.
That's a sure sign of feeling fine.

55

The Source of Life

Are flowers grateful
when rain falls from the sky?
Are trees grateful
when I nuzzle them
with my cheek?

Gratitude is the source of life.
If the natural world
gives us life,
can our love give life
back to the natural world?

56

At Feathered Pipe Ranch

I felt my heart open
looking at the moss on the gray rocks,
the aspen leaves, and the lake.

I love the world!

I love the dirt, the sun, the breeze, and OMG I love the lake.

I love myself, my skin, my bones, my blood vessels, and
whoever it is my spirit holds.

57

Woman in the Cave

When I walk into the cave, there's a woman sitting on the ground by the fire. She invites me to sit down. I tell her I have a present for her, and I hand her something I made, but it has a black cloth over it.

She tells me I can ask her one question. She is Creativity.

"How can I experience more joy in creating and following through with my creations?"

"You must love yourself more deeply. Creating is about loving yourself. It's an expression of loving yourself. You need to love the broken places. It's all about love. Explore yourself through writing. I'm waiting for you, and I'm already here.

"You are not meant to be an 'artist,' but you are meant to love yourself and your life, through play and creating. Get your feet wet. Dig your toes in the sand. Slowly immerse yourself. Writing is a way to discover yourself, but it's not the only way.

"I am already with you. Go home and make love to your life."

58

Who Do I Seek?

Who do I seek?
It's not God.
It's myself.

How do I make my life a creative dance?
A luscious dance?

It's more than, "What do I do in the world?"
I want to love my life.
With feeling.
Not just in my mind.

I know I have a great life, but how do I fully feel that?
How do I wake up to possibility?

I have come so far and worked so hard.
I'm tired.
I need some grace.

How do I share who I am in a healing way?
I have fought the dragon.
I have been tempered by the fire.
I am ready to return home and give back.

I want to live each day with appreciation.
Hold some things sacred.

I want to be the water in the well.
I want a friend who really gets me.
That would be beautiful.

I want to be the person in the future world
ready to catch people
as they stumble disoriented into the new world.

Facing Death
(October 29, 2018–
January 31, 2019)

On October 29, 2018, Eliana had a biopsy that confirmed that the mass on her pancreas, found ten days earlier on a CAT scan, was cancerous. In the recovery room, the surgeon told Eliana she might have only three weeks to live. She lived three more months.

59

Fellow Traveler

While she was visiting and caring for me and before I was too sick, my sister Davia (née Kim) and I went to The Med in Boulder for hot molten chocolate cake and ice cream. It was good, but the chocolate could have been darker. Afterward, Davia wanted to pop into the Boulder Book Store, and I headed back to the car. As I walked down the steps to the underground parking garage, I passed a disheveled young man sitting in the stairwell.

Davia and I had seen the same man lying in a fetal position on the landing when we were on our way to the restaurant. Seeing him there was sad, but we couldn't see his face, so he was a bit easier to ignore. Now he was sitting up, so I stopped, looked him in the eyes, and asked if he needed anything. He said no, but when I got down to the next flight of stairs, I could hear him crying.

Should I go back? He said he didn't need anything, so I continued to my car. Sitting in the driver's seat, I vacillated. *Should* I go back? He might think that's weird after so much time has passed. But what if he's like the Buddha or the Baal

Shem Tov or some other high spiritual being in disguise and this is my last opportunity to be of great service to someone?

I went back upstairs. He was still there, looking desolate.

"I was in my car and thought you shouldn't be sitting here by yourself."

I sat down next to him. It felt so natural to sit close and put my arm around him and rub his back.

He put his face in his hands and cried. After a little while he said, "Thank you. I didn't know if there were any kind, compassionate people left in the world. You give me hope."

His wavy red hair was tangled, and when he looked up at me, his brilliant blue eyes stood out. His face was handsome and bright, but also stressed and sad. I suspected he was homeless because he was wearing socks but no shoes. But when I'd put my arm around him, I had immediately noticed that he didn't smell bad. He was wearing a faded blue long-sleeved T-shirt with a cracked and peeling logo of the Colorado flag.

"What are you doing here?" I asked.

"I'm waiting for her to call."

"Do you have family here?"

"Yeah, they're all here."

As he spoke, I wasn't sure if he was speaking from the same reality that I was living in.

"Are you hungry? Would you like to get some lunch?"

"Yes, I'm very hungry, but I'm too dirty to go anywhere." Then after a beat he said, "Well maybe we could go to a drive-through."

"Okay, let's go."

He came down to my car with me, then we drove to Good Times Burgers where I bought him a meal. We sat together and talked a bit while he ate. It wasn't clear to me if he had mental health issues. I couldn't really tell.

When he finished his meal, I asked, "Do you need some money?"

"No."

"Well, would you *like* some money?"

"Yeah."

It didn't seem as if he was trying to get anything from me. He was polite.

I looked in my wallet and saw that I only had a twenty-dollar bill. I gave him the twenty, which is something I wouldn't have done otherwise—if I weren't dying, that is.

Dying gives you permission to try living a different way.

60

Belonging

I joined Congregation Nevei Kodesh in 1996 when I first moved to Boulder. Over the years, I dropped my membership multiple times, only to rejoin again later. One of the reasons I originally joined a synagogue was that I thought it would be comforting to have a community of people who might care about me if I ever got sick.

For many years I didn't attend services frequently because I didn't want to have to sit alone. I didn't really know anyone, and I figured that nobody knew who I was either. Then one Friday evening, while sitting alone during services and feeling sorry for myself, I privately resolved, "I am going to change my story about this."

I started noticing that some people *did* know my name, and they would greet me with a friendly "Hello, Eliana" when I entered the sanctuary. It dawned on me that it wasn't that the other members didn't know my name, it was that *I* hadn't made an effort to learn *their* names. How can I make friends with people if I don't even know their names? Time to change that.

As I sat in the back row, I went one by one through all the people at temple that night, asking myself, "Might that person like me? Might that person? What about that person?" After considering everyone, I came up with two people who possibly didn't like me. They were the two people whom I most wanted to like me. I previously had a relationship with one of them that had become strained, and I felt a bit intimidated by the other person, although I had always hoped to be her friend.

I decided to tell myself a new story—a simple story that "everybody here loves me." Maybe those two people don't, but everyone else does. At least I decided to choose this as my new story. After services, members typically gather to schmooze and nosh at the Oneg Shabbat. In the past, it was hard for me to mingle and talk with others. But once I began telling myself a new story, I began to feel love for my fellow Nevei Kodesh members.

That inspired me to learn more people's names. I paid close attention each time someone introduced themselves, and whenever I heard a new name, I worked hard to fix it in my brain. Every time I attended services, I'd look around the room and practice silently reciting the names I knew. "That's so-and-so and that's so-and-so." As I learned more names, I began to feel more invested in the community, and I wanted to get more involved.

When they announced they were going to build a new website, I volunteered to help. The process was long and somewhat chaotic. We had multiple meetings, and then the team would change. People would show up, some would disappear, and new people would come, which can be common with volunteer projects. But that gave me the opportunity to meet more people. It felt good to contribute by doing my assignments well and to be appreciated for my efforts.

The next summer I worked in the office for a short stint as an assistant to the executive director, and my circle grew wider. I began to feel like more of an insider and had a better sense of what was going on within the organization. Then I volunteered two consecutive years for the annual fundraiser. I came up with several design ideas for the events and worked on software for the silent auction. I had become increasingly connected to the community.

The Friday after I was diagnosed with terminal pancreatic cancer, Rav Bracha, the rabbi at Nevei Kodesh, announced at Shabbat services that I was ill and probably only had a few weeks to live. People were terribly distressed, and many of them dashed off emails to me expressing their concern. I was touched by their caring but also frustrated that they didn't know my perspective.

I wanted them to know that I was at peace with dying and unafraid. I wrote my own letter directly to the congregation to express this. I also wrote that although I wasn't up for phone calls, emails, or visits, I would enjoy cards from anyone who wanted to let me know how I had affected their lives.

Ask and ye shall receive. Many people wrote that they were inspired by my attitude toward death. Many, many people stepped up and cooked for me and my visiting family those last few months—just as I had hoped a community would care for me if I ever became ill.

It was deeply gratifying to learn that I had positively impacted far more people than I thought. Everybody *did* love me! All because I decided to change my story one Shabbat evening several years before.

61

Oblivious to the Love

Buoyed by the lovely cards I received from Nevei Kodesh congregants in response to my note, I decided to send a similar email to my clients and friends, near and far. I didn't know how much longer I would be alive, and I wanted to reach out to share the news of my diagnosis and that I was at peace with dying.

As I had done in my Nevei Kodesh note, I wrote that I would appreciate a card from anyone who felt inclined to write one. More cards started coming in. Each one was thoughtful, appreciative, and included examples of specific ways I had made a difference. These were things I never would have known. I received more than one hundred cards, and every single one was illuminating.

I was blown away. Not just by the kind things people wrote, but by the impact I apparently had on their lives. I had no idea. I had been totally oblivious. All this time I thought that not that many people really cared about me or even noticed me, and meanwhile, all these people had. That was a huge lesson.

ut that's not all. The letters prompted me to reflect on my lifelong search for purpose. It was sobering to realize how searching for my purpose had, in many ways, become a trap or impediment. While I was in the Moonies, convinced I had found my purpose, I felt trapped into staying because I was so afraid of losing my purpose.

Subsequently, in the four decades since my kidnapping and deprogramming, I had been so focused on finding a grand new purpose that I hadn't noticed the many ways I was impacting others. All because I was too busy trying to figure out how I could make a positive difference in the world!

To anyone haunted by the question of purpose, I offer this deathbed discovery: Make sure your search for purpose isn't an obstacle to living in the present.

62

Perks of Dying

Eliana recorded herself speaking to the camera and sent this as a video message to her extended family.

* * *

My Dear Family,
Thank you so much for all your cards and care packages. I really appreciate them all, and I'm sorry I haven't been taking phone calls. It just takes so much energy to talk on the phone. Since we have not spoken lately, I wanted to give you an update. I have discovered there are lots of perks to dying, so you shouldn't feel bad about me. Let me tell you some of the perks.

<u>Perks of Dying</u>
I don't have to wear sunscreen. Isn't that cool?
I don't have to worry about getting Alzheimer's, and I was really afraid of that.
I don't have to worry about getting cancer because I already have it!

*.. don't have to worry that I'll fall down the stairs, then it
freezes, and I freeze to death because nobody finds me.
I don't have to worry about that guy in the White House.
I don't have to worry about climate change. That's a relief.
Now here's one I bet you never thought about—
I don't have to worry about buying organic.
I can buy the apples with all the pesticides in them.
Because, who cares?*

*So that's my little update, and I want you to know I love you.
I'm so grateful that you're my family. You have been the best
family ever. That's it. Bye.*

*Love,
Eliana*

63

Everything Is Slowing Down

Everything is slowing down. My mind is slower. I am talking slower. I know, I talk slow already. I think slower. I move slower. You know, all that stuff. The only thing I do faster is, oh never mind. (It has to do with bowel evacuation, one of the unpleasant effects of pancreatic cancer.)

What else about my current state? Well, I don't think I'm as funny anymore either. It's too draining. And my mind is slower, so I don't come up with quips easily.

As if in poetic illustration, while speaking, Eliana promptly fell asleep. In her final weeks, she slept a great deal and regularly drifted in and out of sleep during conversation.

Me and my beloved cat Jessie.

64

My Last Goodbye

When Eliana learned of her diagnosis, she met with her rabbi, Tirzah Firestone, seeking guidance and asking if she would officiate at her funeral. In response, Tirzah asked Eliana to write a letter that she, Tirzah, could read on the occasion. This is what Eliana wrote.

* * *

I usually shy away from goodbyes. When I go to a party, I tend to slide out the back door because I'm uncomfortable saying goodbye. And my favorite part of a party is going home.

But this is a monumental goodbye, so I don't want to slide out the back door before I head for my true home. I want to acknowledge the time we have shared together and the love I have for each one of you.

I have never been afraid to die. I've actually been looking forward to it my whole life. When I was ten years old, I sat alone in a field surrounded by a pine forest and had a strong sense that the trees and animals were all connected—as if

319

they were all talking amongst themselves but I couldn't hear. I felt left out and alone. "Maybe when I die," I mused, "I'll be able to talk to the trees. Maybe then I'll feel connected, no longer isolated. I can't wait for that day."

When I recently was told that I didn't have long to live, after my initial shock, I was flooded with relief. Finally, I can get out of here and go talk to the trees. I was hesitant to share my excitement because that's not the expected reaction. I was afraid of what people would think if I said, "I don't want treatment. I'm ready to go."

I didn't need to worry about telling you, though. You have all been unbelievably supportive of me. And although I am at peace with dying, I know it may be a sad and painful time for you. I feel blessed to have shared my life with each of you in a unique way.

I don't want to give the impression that I'm at peace with dying because I've been depressed my whole life. I've been feeling pretty good for the past ten years or so. But I've done my work here, and I'm looking forward to my next adventure.

Boulder has been my home for twenty-five years. Between the majestic landscape and each one of you, this has been a time of deep healing.

Here are some of the things we have shared: skinny-dipping in the river, deep conversations, hikes on the glorious Boulder trails, a shoulder to cry on, making art projects together, playing on the Slip N Slide in my front yard, the key to your house so I could borrow half-and-half even when you weren't home, a WordPress and graphic designers community where everyone always supports one another, working together to save our planet from climate change, and lots of laughing, dark humor, and quirkiness.

To my family, I adore each one of you. Knowing you are always here for me has been the ground I stand on. Picnics, birthday skits, family vacations, ice cream in the summer and chocolate chip cookies in the winter, the Dodgers song, lots of very long phone calls and, of course, the constant guess who's ... so, guess who I ran into on my way to Heaven?

Many of you know I have a birthday tradition. My absolute favorite activity is skinny-dipping in a fresh mountain river or lake. Every year on my birthday, that's what I do. When I jump into that cold water on a hot summer day, my heart swells with love—for the water, trees, rocks, sunshine, and all that surrounds me.

My favorite activity—skinny-dipping in a cold mountain stream.

Maybe my next adventure will be the ultimate skinny-dip into a pool of love, but this time I'll shed not only my clothes but my body as well.

I have one thing left that I've been working on, which I hope will be a meaningful gift to all of you. For the past forty years, I have yearned to make a creative contribution that would have a healing impact on people. I want the efforts I've made to ease my own emotional suffering to be of benefit to others, especially those who have endured depression. I have been writing a memoir, and it doesn't look like I'm going to have time to finish it while I'm alive. But I have a wonderful collaborator and editor who will complete the book for me. I'd say Stacey's my ghostwriter, but in this case, I'm the ghost and she's the writer.

My hope for all of you and for this gorgeous planet that we live on (or that I used to live on) is that you take care of one another and you help heal the planet and the pain we have inflicted on each other. I'll do what I can from the other side to help you out.

I love you and goodbye for now.

Eliana

Acknowledgments

From Eliana

This book would never have seen the light of day without my coauthor and editor, Stacey Stern. When I was diagnosed with terminal cancer and told I had just a few weeks left to live, I hadn't even begun writing the third act of this book. Stacey asked me, "If you could wave a magic wand, what would you like to see happen with your book?"

When I told her that I wanted it to be finished and released, she said we'd figure out a way to make that happen. I started going through old stories, poems, and journal entries, then I handed them over to her. Thank you, Stacey, for making my lifelong dream a reality.

Thanks also to Linda Parks for her beautiful cover design. Linda and I have worked together on design projects for years, and we made a great team.

It doesn't look like I'm going to be around to know who else will help bring this book into the world, so Stacey will thank them for me.

Finally, I'd like to thank my sisters, Davia Rivka, Jan Burns, and Judy Berlfein, the most important people in the world to me. They have believed in me and in this book, and I am deeply grateful for their love.

From Eliana's sister Judy

In Eliana's acknowledgments, she thanks me and my sisters for our faith in this book. In general, that gratitude is deserved. But the full truth is more complex. As Eliana noted, the book had to move full speed ahead once she realized her time was limited. We sisters, however, were consumed with caretaking and planning and emotional upheaval. Organizing and producing a book was fairly low on our list of priorities.

Eliana's determination shined through until the end. She asked, well maybe demanded is more accurate, if we would usher her manuscript through the drafts, layout, publication, and marketing after she was gone. Each of us looked to the other, overwhelmed by the thought of an additional burden. Due to our particular family dynamics, I ended up volunteering to take on that role. It was an emotional roller coaster to accept the responsibility. In the end, I'm honored to have done it.

Not only because I now get to be here offering insight into my sister's life, but also because it forced and allowed me to ask Eliana questions I may have never otherwise posed, answers I needed to shepherd this book to completion. On those December evenings, in her condo in the foothills of the Colorado mountains, when the sun set early and the chill of winter had settled in, we sat across from each other at her dinner table as I grilled her with questions. *Who is your book for? What do you want people to know or gain from it?* And the most unsettling of all for me, *What has depression, a word society casually tosses around as a generic catch-all for struggle, actually felt like in all its grueling detail in your life, Eliana?*

Here we were, two sisters, who had spent our most formative years sleeping side by side in neighboring beds in the same bedroom, horsing around as kids, engaged in deep conversations about life as adolescents, striving always for meaning as adults, and enjoying a connection that comes from a blend of shared life experiences and overlapping strands of DNA. And yet, the gulf between the baby of the family (me) and the older, third-in-a-row-of-four (Eliana), was vast in ways I couldn't fathom. Why was Eliana's world steeped in torment and isolation for so long while I was blessed with a steady diet of general contentment?

As Eliana wrote in her prologue, we all use blinders to help us navigate a world filled with challenges, ugliness, goodness, and beauty. This book provides a connection for me back to my sister, to remember the pain as well as the joy. While we had openly discussed many times over the years the fact that life had treated her more unfairly than it had treated me, I think we both needed to wait until her life was nearing its end for me to grasp the details of her reality. Her immense sadness for prolonged periods had been too much for me to fully acknowledge and digest at the time.

I am thankful that Eliana put her life story down on paper, as stories and journal entries. In her final weeks, as she revisited her journals and other writings, she expressed pride in the bumpy road of progress she had traveled. She was fiercely determined to share this evolution, hoping her lessons would enrich the lives of others.

I am grateful (and I'm sure Eliana is also) for those who participated in the project. Thank you to Mark Gunther and Leslie Schwartz for reading the manuscript and offering helpful insights from an outsider's perspective. Thank you to Davia for working with Eliana to finalize the title and cover art—definitely Davia's strengths, not mine. Thank you to Jan for all things photo-related, for spotting that picture of the Texas deprogramming home that our mother snapped during the long hours spent in the middle of nowhere without much to do, and for making sure the photo made it into the book and not the trash can. Thank you to my husband, Dadla, for stepping in wherever needed with photos, Mailchimp, and editing. Thank you to Stacey for dropping everything when Eliana called at the end of October 2018. Stacey stepped in and spent hours and hours with Eliana, hearing her story, setting her up to record her thoughts, and immersing herself in all of Eliana's journals so she could complete the daunting tasks of compiling act three and accurately editing acts one and two.

And lastly, thank you to Eliana's friends and family, who hung with her during sixty-four years of ups and downs and during her final months filled with both joyous and painful moments, beginning Halloween of 2018 and ending just before Valentine's Day of 2019. Your cards, food deliveries, and calls were greatly appreciated by her and our family. When I spoke with Eliana by phone at the end of December and asked how things were going, she said, "This is the best vacation I've ever been on."

From Stacey

Rabbi Tirzah Firestone, PhD ~ Thank you for suggesting that Eliana contact me to work with her on her memoir. None of us knew at the time that Eliana's terminal diagnosis would soon follow, dramatically altering the trajectory of her life and the nature of our collaboration. When you later acknowledged my completion of what you referred to as "this very karmic, holy task" and added, *Who gets the mystery tugging at our lives?*, I was filled anew with appreciation for the great mystery and your graceful hand in it.

Linda Parks ~ Thank you for designing a whimsical cover that so well reflects our beloved Eliana.

Hynek Palatin ~ Thank you for your interior design, Amazon posting, and abundance of technical and production support. Your professionalism, patience, and generosity are deeply appreciated.

Rivvy Neshama and John Wilcockson ~ You are a dynamic proofreading duo! I am grateful for your exquisite attention to detail and depth of experience.

Judy Berlfein, Jan Burns, and Davia Rivka ~ Thank you for welcoming me and this project into your lives during the most unsettling of times. I have been impressed by your individual talents, familial candor, and collective commitment to caring for Eliana and ensuring that this dream of hers was realized. Extra gratitude to Judy for taking on the family coordinator role and working closely with me.

Eliana ~ I am honored beyond words that you invited me into the final months of your life, turned your personal journals over to me, and boldly engaged in our probing conversations about life and death. I hope you're smiling down from above, feeling peace and joy as the memoir that long lived in your heart is now out in the world.

About the Author

Eliana Berlfein grew up in Los Angeles with her parents, two older sisters, and me (her younger sister, Judy) in a Reform Jewish home. Always looking for ways to distinguish herself from "the Berlfein girls" and discover her unique purpose, Eliana found Reverend Moon's Unification Church and joined in 1975. During her sixth year of devotion to the Church, and shortly after she was matched for marriage by Moon to a fellow Moonie, our parents had her kidnapped and deprogrammed.

Finding her place in the world didn't come easily to Eliana, even before she joined a cult. But after that experience, she struggled intensely to readjust to life without the structure and purpose the Church had provided.

However, Eliana was blessed with an amazing ability to persevere. After decades of struggle, she found peace and relief from depression in the beauty of the Colorado mountains. In her final years, she loved to snuggle with her cat Jessie; craft fantastical, life-size art pieces from papier-mâché and three-dimensional works with polymer clay; swim and go tubing with friends in Boulder Creek; bake peach pies for neighbors; talk, philosophize, and eat ice cream and chocolate chip cookies with her sisters; and be silly with her now grown-up nieces and nephews.

Our family in 2012 shortly before both of our parents died.
From left to right, back row: Davia, Jan, Eliana, Judy;
front row: our mother, Jean, and father, Harold.